Massively Multiplayer Online
Role-Playing Games

Massively Multiplayer Online Role-Playing Games

*The People, the Addiction
and the Playing Experience*

R.V. KELLY 2

McFarland & Company, Inc., Publishers
Jefferson, North Carolina, and London

LIBRARY OF CONGRESS CATALOGUING-IN-PUBLICATION DATA

Kelly, R.V., 1955–
    Massively multiplayer online role-playing games : the people, the addiction and the playing experience / R.V. Kelly 2.
        p.   cm.
    Includes bibliographical references and index.

    ISBN 0-7864-1915-6 (softcover : 50# alkaline paper) ∞

    1. Internet games — Social aspects.   2. Fantasy games — Social aspects.   3. Role playing — Socail aspects.   4. Internet addiction. I. Title.
    GV1469.17.S63K45   2004
    793.93'2 — dc22

                                                            2004017518

British Library cataloguing data are available

Cover illustration by R.V. Kelly 2

Manufactured in the United States of America

McFarland & Company, Inc., Publishers
    Box 611, Jefferson, North Carolina 28640
        www.mcfarlandpub.com

Table of Contents

Introduction: The Appeal of the Unreal   1

1 — Out of the MUD: The Evolution of
    Synthetic Worlds   13
2 — MMORPG Culture   24
3 — The Psychology of MMORPG Players   46
4 — Attraction and Addiction   62
5 — Sampling the Games   100
6 — The Private World of MMORPGs   151
7 — Making a MMORPG   166
8 — The Future of MMORPGs   177

Appendix: Online Addiction Organizations; MMORPG
    Information Sites   193
Bibliography   194
Index   197

Introduction:
The Appeal of the Unreal

"The needs of the body are few, the needs of the spirit many."
— Lao Tzu, *Tao Te Ching*

"Unnatural deeds do breed unnatural troubles."
— William Shakespeare, *Macbeth* V.i.75

2:00 A.M.

Rubbing my inflamed eyes, I realize that I've been staring at the computer screen for 20 straight hours. My back hurts. My head is spinning. My tongue is coated with a gummy rind. I can hardly keep my chin off the keyboard. But I can't go to bed yet. It's only 2:00 A.M. and I have too many important things to do.

Somewhere in the middle of the virtual forest my corpse is rotting away. Its flesh will decay overnight if I don't discover its final resting place, and I'll lose the trinkets that are stored on the cadaver — serious trinkets, important trinkets. I've invested several thousand hours of my life acquiring those arcane oddments and sparkly tchotchkes, so they mean something to me. And I'm not leaving until I find them.

I know other people would see my behavior as ludicrous. They'd either smirk derisively at me or be embarrassed for me. Here is a grown man who is bedazzled by childish electronic doodads, they'd say. He lives in a fantasy world. He's ignoring his family, evading his obligations,

1

ruining his health, and wasting his life playing a game. He's not even paying attention to the needs of his own rancid torso just so he can spend *another* night searching for virtual cadavers. How very sad.

But I probe my conscience to see if this bothers me and, nope, it doesn't. I'm not interested in what other people think. They're not here and I am. It took me months of deliberate planning and careful action to accumulate those possessions. And I'll be grievously unhappy if I lose them.

As I'm searching for my dead self, another hapless soul appears in the dark woods in front of me. He's looking for his mortal remains too. Greeting me, he speaks a language I don't understand, but when I say, "Hiya," he pops into the Mother Tongue.

He turns out to be a Danish middle school teacher who became hooked on the game when his students dared him to try it for a week. That was nine months ago. He says he's already late for a real-world funeral in the suburbs of Copenhagen today, but that the deceased, his uncle, was an avid game player who would understand this reason for his nephew's missing the first half of the funeral service.

Suddenly, the villain who killed us both jumps out from behind a hedge and mutters threats in a deep *basso profundo*. Glowering menacingly and towering over us, he spins the handle of his massive ax. My first impulse is to run. But I can't leave my newfound friend here alone.

The creature's polished silver breastplate glints in the sunlight. I swing wildly at him, bobbing, twisting, and weaving. Trying out some new maneuvers, I stab him in the belly with my dagger.

He knocks me to the ground and raises his weapons, but, just as he is about to separate my head from my body, my new friend launches a series of arrows into the villain's back. All of them find their mark in quick succession. I can hear the thuds as they implant themselves in the meat of the body. The bully drops to the ground, releases a guttural death rattle from his throat, and expires in front of us.

I think to myself, is this violent life good for me? Is this what I should be doing with my time?

My friend spots his own body in a drainage ditch, retrieves his goods, and, with a wave, rushes off to his sad obligations.

3:00 A.M.

Glancing at my real-world surroundings, I see, scattered around the room, scraps of paper recording place names and coordinates, scribbled notes detailing the whereabouts of quest items, hand-drawn maps, a homemade catalog of characters who've helped or harmed me, and shopping lists of items I'm searching for.

My eyes rest on the family dog, who commences a whining lament because I forgot to take him out earlier. A 150-pound Newfoundland is not an animal who should be denied bathroom privileges. But I figure his complaints won't crescendo for a while, so I have a little time before I have to attend to his needs.

I understand his suffering, though. My own insides are about to rupture as well. But any real relief is going to require getting out of my chair. And that won't happen until later. My real body will just have to wait a few more hours. I have more important problems to attend to.

As I re-enter the virtual world, I discover my mortal remains on the crest of a monadnock. But camped around the cadaver are several blood-red and night-black denizens of the rocky alpine regions.

I run in fast and bend down to touch my corpse. I almost have it. There are the trinkets I've been searching for arrayed on the ground in front of me. I reach for them. I lift the first one into the air. And then someone clobbers me in the back of the head with a spiked ebony club.

Instantly I'm inside the tunnel. Dead again. How many times do I have to shuffle off the mortal coil before I realize I'm not invincible?

4:00 A.M.

Reincarnated miles away, I run through the woods back to my two bodies. But I pass a wedding party on the road and stop for a moment to listen to their conversation.

It turns out to be a group of groomsmen and bridesmaids from western Canada debating the effects of a violent virtual life — just the subject I'm interested in.

One of the players says that he fights and kills in the game world all day long, but that doesn't make him a violent person. In fact, he says he's calmer and less violent in real life because he pours his aggressive urges into hurting virtual people instead of hurting real people.

Another character disagrees, suggesting that all the hacking and slashing makes players think, somewhere deep in their brains, that killing is acceptable. So, when they see buildings being bombed or people being shot on TV, they don't flinch or protest because it just seems natural after so much time in the violent game world.

Another character adds that the game gives players the mistaken impression that killing is heroic when, in fact, killing is only destructive. Helping people and selfless devotion to the good of the community are heroic.

Another player chimes in that the game world makes the death of a living creature something to laugh at, even celebrate. It has a biological effect while you're doing it. Adrenaline pumps through you when something attacks, and when you kill it, endorphins surge through you in relief. So, you feel good about killing. And you're not just watching the murders happen on TV. You're committing them. You're learning to take a visceral pleasure in destroying living creatures.

Intrigued because I've been pondering the same issues, I act as if I'm part of the wedding party and say, "There was a famous case a few years ago in Massachusetts where a kid who had just gotten his driver's license went out for a first drive with his girlfriend. This kid was a rabid gamer and, when he saw a classmate that he didn't like on the street, he aimed right for him. He sped up and struck the kid headfirst and killed him. He yelled out, 'All right! Ten points!' as his victim went under the car. The girlfriend saw the whole thing."

The others have mixed opinions about this account. They defend themselves by saying that there are some mentally unstable individuals who might do such a thing, but that you can't paint all gamers with the same brush. Most people can distinguish between the real world and the game world.

Before I can hear the rest of their responses, though, I'm already running. I can't wait. I'm driven by an inner obsession. Maybe I'm one of those mentally unstable individuals, I think. I have important things to do. But none of them are in the real world.

5:00 A.M.

When I glance at the clock I see it's 5:00 A.M. The sky outside is beginning to brighten. I've been up all night. My ears are ringing. My legs are severely cramped. My head is wilting on a sore neck. I'm inches from sleep. I'm moving in bleary slow motion. The bear growling in my belly and the now-quite-extreme preeruption-geyser pressure in my intestines are telling me that it's time to do something else for a while, something healthy, something life-affirming.

But I've learned to ignore my own physical complaints. The needs of the real body come second. I have more important things to worry about than bursting bladders, sleep deprivation-induced psychosis, and a stomach beginning to digest its own lining. I'm focused on what's important in life — the game. I'm using the simple binary logic of the addict. Retrieving my belongings from a heap of corpses is critical. Everything else is meaningless.

Jumbuck, my polysyllabic son, age 14, comes down to the cellar where the computer is to see if he can do a little exploring in the desert badlands. He snorts when he sees me trapped in the forest.

"Please don't inform me that you've been ensconced here all night," he moans.

Sadly, this is not the first time I've done this.

"Whoa," he says, looking at my bodies stacked like firewood. "Not much sense in provoking your demise again. Maybe sympathetic altruists will meander by to proffer assistance."

And, as he says this, lo and behold, a contingent of early risers comes tramping through the dappled forest on their way to a quest beyond the distant snowy peaks.

"Sorry to bother you!" I broadcast to the group before they get away. "Any chance of some help?"

Without a word of command, the group launches into an attack on the creatures. The archers enfilade the swarm from where they're standing. The sword and mace men bound into the melee, khanjars and morning stars swinging. When the smoke clears, all of the villains are defeated.

But, as I busy myself with robbing my own grave, one of the players asks if anyone here is from France. He says he's flunking French in high school because he's been on the game too much and he needs a tutor, someone who could talk to him only in French while he's in the game world.

The group members identify themselves as two Englishmen, a Czech, a Dutch woman, an Irish boy, and a girl from Quebec. The girl says she'll help but then cautions him that most of the words he's going to learn will probably be about death and monsters.

Going about my business, I retrieve the goods stored on each corpse and drag my battered self away from the pile of cadavers. Then, overburdened, knuckle-walking, chastened, and grateful, I wish everyone well and scramble hastily out of the morbid realms to more clement climes in the valley below.

6:00 A.M.

Then I stand up for the first time in 24 hours.

I can feel the blood rushing to my numb feet. My legs will barely unfold. My wrists ache with carpal tunnel nerve swelling. My eyes are smoldering from the equivalent of three contiguous workdays of staring at the computer screen. I don't dare look in a mirror. I know crimson scleras will glow hauntingly back at me. Either that or miniature whirling pinwheels.

"Don't touch anything!" I yell as I leave the room now redolent of my scent. "I'm coming right back here! Don't touch anything!"

But when I return from the ineffable ecstasy of relief, my 11-year-old daughter, Bunyip, has taken her place at the computer. She's playing her character and will not be shifted.

"Nobody was here, so I'm taking my hour now!" she shouts.

I need to get some sleep. I know I do. But I don't want to leave the land of treacherous circumstance, virulent monsters, and charitable samaritans. I can't leave yet. There's too much left to do.

I wobble unsteadily in the doorway. My eyes well up. My knees quiver. I know the right thing to do is to go to bed before I fall down. But I'm not willing to vacate a world I've inhabited every day for more than a year and for up to twenty-four hours a day, a world that means more to me than real life does.

I consider tricking her out of the seat. But I can't think clearly enough to formulate a plan. Even in my foggy, wild-eyed, confused state, I realize something is wrong with my thought processes. It has to be exhaustion. Either exhaustion alone or exhaustion mixed with something more sinister. Addiction maybe.

As if she can read my mind, Bunyip plants herself firmly in the chair like a brave protestor determined to be dragged from the building by the police. I struggle with my baser impulses, clenching my hands, blinking my eyes, trying to concoct some way to get myself back into the virtual world.

I can see the armor-clad characters running through the shady woods. I can hear the roar of the monsters. I want to get back in there. But she's oblivious to my needs. Everyone is. Don't they understand? Why won't they get out of my way?

My eyes are closing as I stand in the doorway. Before I collapse, I trudge reluctantly upstairs to bed.

I climb in, but my thoughts linger in the universe of malevolent forests, infested dungeons, and corpse-strewn prairies. As I slide under the blanket I disturb Brumby, my wife, who turns to ask, "Getting up so early? I didn't even hear you come in last night. When did you finally get to bed?"

I'm asleep before I can respond. But the notion of addiction haunts my bubbling, furious, psychedelic, monster-fleeing, fabulous-wealth-accumulating, powerful-now-and-soon-to-be-unconquerable, is-that-the-newest-sword? anyone-know-where-a-good-place-to-croak-golems-is? how-did-I-become-locked-into-this-world? why-am-I-acting-this-way? what-do-I-gain-from-this? what's-wrong-with-me? dreams.

Quicksand

Before I had entered a MMORPG (Massively Multiplayer Online Role-Playing Game — pronounced, rather ominously, morgue) for the first time, all I knew about them was that some players had developed a compulsion for them. In fact, people had become so addicted to them that they had suffered withdrawal symptoms — cravings, irritability, and obsessive thoughts — when they had to leave. But I could not for the life of me imagine why.

What could anyone possibly see on a computer screen that would hold his attention for 18 hours a day? How could someone spend every night for years staring at a monitor and clicking a mouse? How could anyone become addicted to an activity that completely separated them from the pleasures of the tangible world? And why would anyone abandon real life to immerse themselves in an invented universe?

I now know why all of these things happen. Through experience I've learned about the pleasures and pitfalls of life in a realm that is not only less painful than the real world, but in many ways richer, more sensible, more beautiful, more satisfying, more interesting, and more intensely real.

How was I converted? It happened by accident.

A friend of mine works for a company that builds MMORPGs. I wanted Jumbuck to see what life was like in an organization devoted to virtual world production, so I arranged a visit.

We strolled into the company's dimly lit warehouse-style production building. Jumbuck's eyes widened. We passed programmers lounging in beanbag chairs on the floor, tapping code into keyboards resting on their laps. We strolled by artists drawing well-armored characters in heroic stances with biceps and breasts shaded to impressive comic book proportions. And everything was fine until my friend, Les, called us over to his computer.

Lifting his hands to block the face of the screen as if he were shielding us from the Medusa's countenance, he warned us that the game was highly addictive. In the serious voice of a drug counselor, he told us not to look at it unless we were willing to take that chance.

I had to laugh. I mean, puh-leez. It's one thing to take your job seriously. It's quite another to assume that you're working on something that will so infect the minds of the weak-willed saps viewing it that they will sink into the Slough of Despond if deprived of its seductive radiance in the future. It's a *game*, for Pete's sake. It's a slightly more evolved version of *Pong* and *Pac-Man*. Little cartoon critters move around on the monitor. One bunch of electrons hits another bunch. They make squeaky noises. They're not going to capture anyone's soul or change anyone's life. And they certainly wouldn't have any effect on me.

I smirked. "I think we'll risk it." And we sat down to watch a little man in jousting attire run through a meadow.

The epiphany was stunning, powerful, and immediate. I looked at the screen. And, all at once, my view of myself shifted. I became a gamer. There was no gradual building of subterranean pressure that would lead to a later tectonic shift, no subtle grinding of crustal plates. The earthquake struck immediately and without warning. And it was a 9.9 on the Richter scale.

I had been one person before, gazing into a new world. And I became another person when I tried to turn away and couldn't.

This isn't a game at all, I realized. It's a vast, separate universe with its own rules, constraints, culture, ethos, ethics, economy, politics, and inhabitants. People explore here. They converse. They transact business, form bonds of friendship, swear vows of vengeance, escape from dire circumstance, joke, fight to overcome adversity, and learn here. And it's *better than the real world* because there are no physical consequences for making mistakes. You can derive the same sense of satisfaction for doing things well that you find in the real world, but you don't suffer any pain or anguish when you fail. So, the game contains most of the good found in real life, but none of the bad.

By the time we'd left the building, I had decided to subscribe to the monthly game service, and Jumbuck noticed an odd change in his father's demeanor. On the one hand, this change was encouraging. Finally, Dad seemed to comprehend a key element in the true meaning of life. But, on the other hand, it was slightly unsettling because there was no telling how such a fundamental shift in the workings of the universe would unfold.

I wasn't worried, however.

I had done virtual reality R&D work at the erstwhile Digital Equipment Corporation for seven years, along with another dozen years working elsewhere in artificial intelligence, artificial life, distance learning, computational biology, and interactive TV. So I had enough history in these fields to see my entry into the game world as a form of research.

When I saw the little men and women running through the forest on the computer screen, I recognized a chance to observe people from all parts of the planet cooperating inside an enormous virtual laboratory.

And the game world was astonishingly similar to the virtual worlds I was accustomed to building, so I was anxious to jump in and start taking notes.

What I had seen in my VR work was that the inhabitants of new worlds tended to go through three stages of development. First, they embarked on missions of discovery. Then they set out to destroy what they saw around them. Then they got creative and rearranged their environment. Almost everyone went through the same three stages in a virtual world, some quickly, some slowly, some dwelling on one or going back to another, but always, strangely, in the same order. I wanted to see if this exploration, destruction, and creation sequence was the same in the MMORPG world.

I also wanted to confirm my old observation that people preserved their real worldview while in the virtual world. I had found that if they were distrustful of others in real life, that distrust did not drop away when they entered a synthetic world. If they were garrulous and affable in real life, they were garrulous and affable in virtual life too. In fact, the virtual world often magnified their existing personalities.

And I'd noted that if people stayed together in the virtual world long enough, they began to develop a unique culture and slang that gradually distinguished them from people in the outside world. They christened virtual places with interesting names. They used old words in new ways to describe their strange surroundings. They evolved traditions through repetition, and turned funny events into inside jokes and, eventually, into idioms. A culture evolved naturally among inhabitants in a virtual world, independent of anything the world's developer might have intended.

I wanted to investigate all of these areas in the MMORPG universe, and more. So, when the package arrived, I logged in and immersed myself immediately. In fact, I immersed myself so deeply that I entered a kind of hypnotic trance. I looked up from the screen and noticed that it was four hours later than when I had sat down. If not for hunger pangs and bathroom urges I would have had no connection to the real world for the entire day. This was the start of the slippery slope.

In no time at all, I had all but abandoned real life in favor of the virtual realm. It was like being pulled down by an undertow at the beach and dragged out to the middle of the ocean. I couldn't resist the tug.

But I learned something on the way out to the briny depths about the nature of reality. I learned about the people who discard real life to inhabit a richer world limited only by imagination. And, by interviewing hundreds of other MMORPG players in dozens of games over a three-year period, I learned what it was like to live inside a novel as it was being written and dwell in a new, better, more satisfying universe as it was being created.

—— *Chapter 1* ——

Out of the MUD: The Evolution of Synthetic Worlds

"Reality is merely an illusion, albeit a very persistent one."
— Albert Einstein

"Reality is nothing but a collective hunch."— Lily Tomlin

Massively multiplayer online role-playing games are the newest phenomena in electronic game development, and they are as different from ordinary video games as television is from radio. They're not really games at all, in fact. They're living, self-contained, global, three-dimensional virtual worlds, each one the size of a real-world country filled with forests, prairies, oceans, beaches, mountains, towns, and thousands of simultaneous players.

In MMORPG realms, living human beings not only create new versions of themselves but also collectively evolve new societies. MMORPG dwellers develop moral codes to subtly guide and govern the actions of their fellow inhabitants. They evolve their own patois. They devise their own private economies. And, over time, they invent a separate culture filled with bullying, lying, and criminality on the one hand, and healing, teaching, and magnanimity on the other.

Ordinary players typically spend 20 to 30 hours a week in these worlds, but obsessed players spend every night, every weekend, every vacation — for *years* at a time — forgoing sleep, food, and real human companionship just to experience more time in the virtual world. MMORPGs have, in fact, acquired such a reputation for addicting players that they're regularly referred to as "electronic crack" and "heroin-ware." Even people who have never played a video game in their lives have developed obsessions powerful enough that they've suffered genuine anguish when they've had to leave their game worlds. And some truly addicted players have watched their marriages dissolve, lost their jobs, dropped out of college, and all but abandoned their families because of their compulsion for a new life inside the computer.

Luckier players, however, have derived great benefits from the time they've spent in MMORPG worlds. They've found true love, eventually marrying in real life the partners they learned to love in the game. They've discovered the antidote to real-world shyness and disappointment inside the pixel universe. And they've recognized previously unrealized talents within themselves, found freedom from physical disabilities, or developed a sense of control, purpose, achievement, confidence, and happiness in their lives through participation in the games.

Some of these MMORPG players entered the game realm because they were attracted to a particular setting, usually medieval or otherworldly. Others were fascinated by the lore and rituals. Many players delighted in the sense of accomplishment they experienced when their characters started out feeble, bumbling, and poor, and slowly became strong, adept, and rich. Others were drawn in by the excitement of exploring new territories or nearly being killed twenty times a day. And some players entered the game world to socialize with people from around the world, or even to *hurt* people from around the world without getting hurt themselves.

All of these varieties of attraction may explain why the number of MMORPG players is growing so fast. (It's expected to reach 100 million by the end of the decade.) They may also explain why the games are now redefining the fields of commerce, law, and human interaction.

For example, MMORPGs are now *big* business. A complex MMORPG may cost $2 million to $10 million to build and may take years to develop. But this can be a worthwhile investment because MMORPG audiences now rival those of television shows. More than 3 million people, for example, have played the game Lineage. Just as many people have played Ragnarok Online. One and a half million people have played EverQuest. Games such as Ultima Online, Dark Age of Camelot, Final Fantasy XI, and Star Wars Galaxies now have more than a quarter million players each. And every player pays a monthly fee (usually $9–$15) to remain in the game world, often for years. So, the sums generated by MMORPGs now run into the *billions* of dollars.

And the money that changes hands every year between the players and the developers is matched by the vast sums exchanged between the players themselves. One of the ways, in fact, that MMORPGs fundamentally differ from video games is that MMORPG players can sell their virtual characters and goods for real currency. And the auction sites that have sprung up all over the Internet designed specifically for game items now host such a huge volume of transactions that the sale of virtual objects and characters has become a noteworthy component of global e-commerce.

When the economist Edward Castronova of California State University, Fullerton, for example, calculated the value of EverQuest goods sold through Internet auctions, he found, remarkably, that the game's per capita GDP made the virtual country of Norrath the 77th largest economy in the world — somewhere between the economies of Russia and Bulgaria. He determined that the unit of currency used in the game (which has more than 400,000 current players) is actually more valuable than the real-world Japanese yen or Italian lira.

And other popular games have similar values associated with their items and characters. Trade in virtual goods, in fact, increases every year even though the big unresolved legal question is still, "Who owns the virtual characters created by MMORPG players: the players themselves or the companies that make the game worlds?"

This is an important question because MMORPGs are now sizeable enough as economic entities that they've begun forcing the development of new legal definitions for property, work, and ownership. This legal precedent-setting started when Sony first forbade players from selling their EverQuest game characters and then negotiated a special contract with eBay to prevent those sales. The debate sparked up again when NCSoft banned 200,000 accounts from Lineage for out-of-game trading and was supported by the Korean court system which claimed that NCSoft, not the players, owned all characters created by players in the game.

None of this put a dent in the trade in virtual items, however, because players in most games routinely ignore the bans. Most players, in fact, see restrictions on farming (building characters and collecting virtual items for real-world sale) as inane. They argue that a game company claiming to own player-created characters is the equivalent of a word-processing-software company claiming to own all the books written with its software or a saxophone manufacturer claiming to own all the songs played through its instruments.

As a result of these player attitudes, many games now not only allow but heartily encourage the shadow economy that grows up around them. One company in Sweden, in fact, has even incorporated the idea of player-owned items into its game engine, requiring players to buy directly from the game company the items used inside the game world (clothing, armor, weapons, ammunition, etc.) for real dollars. If players then progress in the game and discover rare loot on monsters, they can sell it back to the game company for cash.

But it's not just commerce and law that have been affected by MMORPGs. So many people have become immersed in the game worlds that MMORPGs are now also a societal force affecting large-scale patterns of human behavior. And this is redefining life in some parts of the world.

In South Korea, for example, the games are popular enough that television ratings plummet when people abandon the tube in favor of game life. Television stations have fought back by creating TV shows featuring people actually playing online games against each other in live contests.

The games are even pervasive enough now that they are perceived as a public health threat in some quarters. In the summer of 2003, for example, the Thai government banned nighttime online game-playing altogether. Countless reports of children who had become addicted to the games worried them. And the curfew was prompted by reported cases of dedicated players who had suffered physical harm as a result of deep vein thrombosis (blood clots in the legs that broke off and caused heart attacks — until now a problem known primarily by long-distance airline passengers forced to sit motionless for too long). The case of Kim Kyung-jae, the 24-year-old South Korean man who died after playing Lineage for 86 hours straight, was well known at the time, so Thai gamers understood the law's intent. But thousands of gamers nonetheless promptly called for the resignation of the government minister responsible for the ban (as also happened in Greece in 2002, when all electronic games were banned there under Law 3037).

On top of these large-scale phenomena have to be added the individual cases of tragedy that are now associated with MMORPGs. Jay Parker, cofounder of Internet/Computer Addiction Services in Redmond, Washington, treated one patient, a 21-year-old college student who, after 36 straight hours of game play, had suffered a psychotic break from sleep deprivation and ran through his neighborhood hallucinating that game characters were after him. In 2001, Shawn Woolley, a 21-year-old avid MMORPG player in Wisconsin, killed himself apparently after being spurned by a female player in EverQuest. His mother filed suit against Sony as a result. In 2000, Tony Lamont Bragg of Florida was accused of throwing his nine-month-old son into a closet because the child disturbed his MMORPG game playing. The boy, who had been severely squeezed to keep him quiet, died of internal bleeding after 24 hours, and the game-playing father was given 15 years in prison after pleading guilty to aggravated manslaughter.

Huge numbers of game players have also become so addicted to their pursuit of the virtual life that they've suffered losses in the real world in the areas of job, school, and family. And the phenomenon is so widespread that there are now several organizations devoted to MMORPG addiction.

All of these new areas — new business models, new legal precedents, new prospects for making money, and new public health concerns — suggest that MMORPGs are more than just a simple game technology. They're a way of expanding our collective sense of possibility, a way of redefining not only ourselves but the real world around us. And, as the number of available MMORPGs increases, our chances of changing both ourselves and society with this technology are growing rapidly.

But where did these powerful games come from? And how did they become so addictive that they've changed the lives of players, forced the legal system to adapt, made billions for their developers, and worried public health officials?

The Deep Past

The origins of high-imagination gaming stretch all the way back through prehistory to the hunting tales told around Cro-Magnon campfires. And those ancient roots may actually explain some of the innate appeal of the games.

The walls of the world-famous Lascaux Cave in France, for example, are profusely illustrated with the same kinds of beasts, weapons, and dead hunters found in many MMORPGs. Erudite gamers joke that these images actually represent the graphical user interface for a 17,000-year-old form of role-playing game. The dashes, dots, and colored squares on the cave walls even look like the indicators used to keep track of health, stamina, and skill points in a MMORPG.

The backers of this not-entirely-humorous proposal suggest that ancient players hunted the painted animals in pantomime while recounting their imagined exploits to the assembled tribe. Veteran hunters, preparing for a new season, used the game to put themselves into the proper frame of mind. Adolescents, anticipating their first big hunt, rehearsed their roles inside the game cave. And those with a penchant for religious practice may even have glorified the game into a spiritual ritual that revolved around a group story-telling effort.

Whether this particular proposition is valid or not, the collaborative story circle method that it points to is among the oldest of human art forms and is certainly part of the ancestry of MMORPGs as well. Some cultures, in fact, still use participatory tale-telling of this kind to entertain themselves, so we know how it works.

In West Africa, for example, one person may act as the central narrator in an antiphonal tale, calling out the main plot points of a story while the other participants respond with, "I was there, and this is what I saw!" The group members then add their own elements to the evolving chronicle knitted aloud by the entire group.

In a more graphical form, this is exactly what happens in MMORPGs, as well, where thousands of players collectively weave, via their behavior and conversation, a story guided by the developers.

But also informing the development of MMORPGs have been the heroic tales of adventure that have been recited for thousands of years in every culture in the world. Tales similar to the legends of the Ronin, the sagas of Leif Ericson, the Camelot stories, the Ramayana, and the recounted voyages of Odysseus, Gilgamesh, and Noah have been retold for millennia. And these too are part of the heritage of MMORPGs because the plots of MMORPG games include the very same narrative elements as the ancient sagas: courage in the face of fear, creative solutions to problems, perseverance under adversity, the exploration of distant places, and triumph over evil.

Usually intermixed with these tales are myths of dragons, demons, giants, magic lamps, flying carpets, hammer-wielding thunder gods, trolls, leprechauns, goblins, and sorcerers — the very elements found in MMORPGs. So it's no wonder that MMORPGs — which tap into a very deep and abiding aquifer of ancient story elements — would become so popular so quickly.

Despite the deep roots, however, the recent precursors of MMORPGs are easy to identify. And one has only to study the history of games over the last 30 years to find the direct progenitors.

D&D and MUDs

Massively multiplayer online role-playing games are the direct offspring of two very modern parents, and from each of these parents they have inherited a particular set of genes that influence how the games are designed and played.

The spiritual father of MMORPGs is the venerable role-playing game Dungeons and Dragons (D&D) — a game that allows players to immerse themselves in the travails of questing knights, clever damsels, and infrahuman forest dwellers.

Itself a descendent of both participatory storytelling circles and ancient folklore, D&D is a way of reenacting the chivalric tales of valor and magic that for hundreds of years enriched the lives of Europeans. In the 1890s, the novelist William Morris wrote a series of books designed to evoke the same intent and feeling as the Knights of the Round Table sagas he had grown up with. In the 1940s, his literary disciple, J.R.R. Tolkien, perfected this genre once known as heroic romance and later called fantasy fiction. And, in keeping with the same ethos, Gary Gygax and Dave Arneson then invented Dungeons and

Dragons in the 1970s as a way of acting out these kinds of fantasy adventures in real time.

To start a D&D session, several players physically meet in the same room, each adopting the role of a different archetypal figure. One person might become a cleric, for example, another a rogue, and the other players fighters, wizards, humans, dwarves, halflings, or elves.

The constraints of a written adventure are then applied onto a generic game board, establishing what kinds of experiences these players will have as they traverse the imaginary world.

The player who reads and interprets this adventure serves as the Dungeon Master (DM) — the director of operations for the game. And, as each player in the room takes a turn traveling the imaginary landscape of the board and acting in character, the Dungeon Master looks at the guidelines stated in the adventure and presents the players with their options. The DM might say, for example, "The door you are trying to open is locked. What do you want to do?" or "You see three attackers in front of you. How do you want to deal with them?"

Players check the abilities of the characters they're playing and then call out what their characters will do next: enter the room, run away, or fight. The group then moves through the adventure dodging traps, circumventing evil creatures, and retrieving treasures.

From Dungeons & Dragons, MMORPGs have inherited not only the spirit of Arthurian romance, but also the notion of adopting a character role with its own defined traits, abilities, and limitations. The D&D character you play, for example, may be particularly skilled at tinkering or sword-swinging, but utterly inept as an archer. And MMORPGs use this same system of character definition.

From D&D also, MMORPGs derive the ideas of progress through a landscape fraught with peril, as well as the various systems for keeping track of a character's health and powers while wandering through a dangerous land dodging or confronting attackers.

Not all MMORPG traits come from D&D though.

The mother of MMORPGs is a different type of game entirely. It's the MUD (Multiple-User Dimension, Dungeon, or Domain) that began in the late 1970s when almost all of the work done on computers was textual rather than graphical.

The earliest MUDs were walk-through text adventures centered on castles and dungeons that housed creatures the player could interact with through written commands. The commands were simple. The responses from the computer were just as simple. And the MUD program's job was to keep track of each character's position, gear, points, accomplishments, and movements in a virtual world portrayed entirely in words.

Information exchanges between player and machine looked like rapid-fire conversations, and the program would show both the commands the player was issuing and the responses made by the computer. For example:

(Player) Turn south.
(Computer) You see a rat.
Look north.
You see a door.
Look west.
There is a beetle.
Fight beetle.
You kill beetle.
Look east.
You see a dungball.
Wield dungball.
You raise dungball off the ground.
Eat dungball.
Dungball restores 15 points of your stamina.

In the mid–1980s, a cousin of this type of MUD game began to appear in which the player organized the birth, health, death, and work assignments of myriad laborers, farmers, artisans, researchers, and military characters. These became some of the first e-mail games.

Every few days, this kind of program would send out turn sheets to all of the players participating in "the collective hallucination," providing all players with information on the state of the game universe.

One player's turn sheet might say, for example,

On Planet 18 you have 465 inhabitants, 720 tons of food, 8.2 million credits, and 16 light-class ships. Your defenses are rated 7. Your probe recognizes a new planet at 45 37 91. Pirates have removed all cargo from your ship at 17 81 82 ...

After a day's digestion of all the new information and plot moves — often totaling 20 or more pages — each user would then send back written e-mail instructions to the game engine, such as:

Launch probe to coordinates 23 45 16.
Attack pirate ship at 19 37 89.
Boost defense level on Planet 9.
Grow 400 tons of food on Planet 73.
Breed 76 people on Planet 12 ...

The computer acted as an electronic Dungeon Master — a coordinator of the events. It processed the weekly instructions of the many players, calculated the consequences of their actions, and sent the individually tailored results to every person playing the game.

Because these games were usually played at the rate of one or two turns a week, a single game could last for years. And the real identities of the participants were never revealed during the game.

This whole notion of players who never saw each others' human forms because the computer acted as a mediator of all interactions between players in the game universe was borrowed by MMORPGs. And, from these same text adventures, the idea of participating in a virtual experience with no definite ending began to take root.

The e-mail-based games that retained their focus on the management of resources and populations evolved into RTS (real-time strategy) games like Age Of Empires and Civilization. Such games preserved the idea of one player creating and controlling thousands of nameless characters who acted in different roles for the good of the society. A game player in this kind of world was a director of the action, rather than an actor. And, in these games, the player took on a divine role by creating anonymous characters who collected gold, wood, and stone to build towns and to feed themselves while occasionally storming the castles of computer-generated opponents.

The real-time one-person-becomes-one-character MUDs, meanwhile, slowly developed graphical front-ends and primitive GUIs (graphical user interfaces) to get beyond the limitations of text. Over time, these evolved into standalone RPGs (role-playing games) such as Final Fantasy and The Legend of Zelda. And then in the late 1990s, when Ultima Online, EverQuest, and Asheron's Call appeared, MMORPGs began to bring these adventures into the global virtual world.

There is one distinct vestige of MUDs, in fact, that is still found in most MMORPGs. It's called chat spew. When you give a command to a MUD it returns a message saying, for example, "Your sword swings. You hit the creature, doing 45 points of damage." In a MMORPG these words are not really necessary, but you usually see them anyway. You swing your sword or fire your laser with a mouse click and the effects of the attack are obvious on the animated image. In most games, though, you still get the ancient MUD-style text message that tells you what you've done.

Each of these modern and ancient precursors of MMORPGs enriches them and brings to them something they would not otherwise have. MMORPGs, for example, contain the narrative elements of ancient myths and legends. They use the same participatory techniques as story-telling circles. They capture the feeling of direct action found in D&D. They connect players to an electronic world, as MUDs do. And, at the same time, they add the sound, movement, and fast pace of traditional blast-or-be-blasted console games. Maybe this combination of the most addictive features of other forms of story-telling and gaming is what makes MMORPGs so incredibly enticing.

—— *Chapter 2* ——

MMORPG Culture

"The life which is unexamined is not worth living."— Plato

"The world is full of people whose notion of a satisfactory future is, in fact, a return to the idealised past."
— Robertson Davies

Entering a MMORPG is like entering a separate universe with its own physical and sociological rules. It's a recognizable universe. You can't walk through walls, for example. And you don't fall upward when you slip. But it's also a wholly different universe. If a rock lands on your head, you feel no pain. And if you cast a spell on yourself, you can fly, or breathe underwater, or shoot lightning bolts from your fingertips. So MMORPGs are simultaneously identical to the real world and completely different from it.

The biggest difference, however, is in the culture, not the physics, of MMORPG realms. And the disparity between the two planes of existence really comes down to certain life-enriching features that MMORPGs possess and that the real world just can't compete with. These unique features define MMORPG society and make the MMORPG universe a fascinating and compelling place to live in.

First among them is certainly the idea of daily progress — something that is taken for granted in every MMORPG but can be conspicuously absent in real life. Then there's the whole concept of the quest, the idea that experience and profit can best be gained by actively seeking out danger. Then, to support the people who are trying to make their way through quests and through the rest of the game world, there are guilds, organizations that work for the betterment of their members. Both quests and guilds are intertwined with the private economies that spring up in all MMORPGs and lead to a good deal of the villainous behavior that taints MMORPG life. And, last, is the practice of player killing that offers everyone the chance to murder other people with impunity. Interlaced through all of these ideas, though, is the concept of guaranteed protection from catastrophe — a feature that most people would like to add to the real world and which has a major effect on MMORPG culture in every game.

A Quick Primer

The first thing anyone does when they enter a MMORPG is cobble together an in-game persona, called an avatar, toon, or character — a little man, woman, alien, or mythical creature that is directed through the game world to explore, trade, negotiate, collect, and do battle. The process of devising this character is like creating a second self. And the use of a unique character created by the player, rather than a one-size-fits-all generic sprite provided by the game's developers, distinguishes MMORPGs from ordinary video games.

The character creation process begins with choosing a character's race — its species, physiognomy, history, heritage, philosophy, and disposition. The types of available races vary from game to game. But they usually include large thoughtless bruisers, clever sylphid waifs, stout determined pugilists, greedy business types, and contemplative spiritual adepts.

Once you've decided on your character's background, you then tweak its appearance. For human characters, this means selecting skin color, haircut, height, weight, and tattooing. For other species, it can mean choosing spaniel ears, a nose long enough to stir soup with, uber-babe lips, ultra-dude reflective sunglasses, a paunchy belly, a furry back, scales, fins, tentacles, you name it. The selection of both male and female characters is allowed and the choice of gender never limits the skills of the character in any way.

Once you've settled on an appearance, you next figure out your profession or class—the way you want your character to handle the challenges of life. Almost all games include some kind of mage who casts spells or uses "mental energy," a melee character who fights hand to hand, and a ranger character who shoots arrows, flings darts, or throws deadly axes. But beyond these common themes the professional possibilities are as wide as they are in the real world. You may be able to become a biotechnician, for example, or a banker, animal trainer, metaphysician, dancer, healer, engineer, thief, miner, bounty hunter, or arbitrageur, depending on the game.

After you've chosen your profession, the selection process then focuses on skills. These are the talents and abilities that allow you to perform specialized actions. They're the abilities that you practice and improve over the long life of your character, the combination of traits that make you successful in the virtual world and distinguish you from everyone else.

Most folks would probably choose every skill available from ocean fishing to armor tinkering, dragon taming, gourmet cooking, acrobatics, dowsing, shape-shifting, meditation, x-ray vision, birdsong imitation, hypnosis, weaving, asteroid mining, lyre plucking, piracy, confidence scheming, rabbit breeding, nursing, and all the rest. But you're only given so many skill credits to distribute between your various abilities. So, you start out reasonably proficient at only a few skills and embarrassingly deficient in all the others. Then, as you use your skills, you gain points that can be employed to improve existing skills and gain new ones.

Finally, you have to invent a name for your character. Some players are so impatient to get started that they leave typos in their names. They have handles like Lime Germlin, Sowrd of Death, and The Balck Shadow.

But most players take the time to dwell on the spelling and meaning of their monikers because, in a strange way, a character's name seeps into the player over time. In fact, it seems to be a common view among MMORPG players that if you call yourself something like Frightened Paranoid and spend thousands of hours living under that alias, you can brand your psyche with a subliminal message that stains your waking consciousness. In their eyes, it's better to call your character Selfless Hero or Oceans of Bliss.

Once your character is completed, it's then time to enter the

MMORPG world to encounter the game's three types of animate beings: PCs, NPCs, and Creatures.

Player Characters (PCs) are the avatars of the other players, the people with whom you can chat, trade, and buddy up. These are the characters who will either selflessly help you out of a jam if you're lucky, or cheat you in a business deal and then kill you if you're not.

Non-Player Characters (NPCs) are the computer-generated figures who facilitate game play. They act as shopkeepers, teachers, guides, or quest initiators. Usually, you click on them to start a conversation or purchase their goods, choosing products or responses from the menus they present.

And Creatures, the third type of virtual world denizen, are the source of both danger and wealth in the MMORPG realms. They can kill you — in which case you may reincarnate somewhere else in the world, lose points, or have to return to your body to collect the dropped items on your cadaver. Or you can kill them — and their dead bodies will provide you with the loot you need to prosper in the game world: weapons, tools, money, clothing, musical instruments, machine parts, gems, potions, and other booty. (In many games you can also tame creatures and ride them or train them to hunt for you.)

Every little success you have in dealing with the three types of inhabitants results in the accumulation of experience points (XP). These are what cause your character to grow and improve over time. And they're why many players stay in the game world for months or years.

If you make restorative medicines, for example, you receive experience points. If you complete a quest handed to you by an NPC, you also gain points. And if you remove a dangerous creature from the landscape, you gain still more points.

Every time you cast a spell, build a forge, heal a friend, or tame a monster, you gain XP. And the more difficult the task, the more points you receive for accomplishing it. The total number of accumulated points then determines your level in the game. (With 1,000 points you may be a Level 2. With 1,000,000 points you'd be a Level 22.) So, when other players scan your approaching avatar, they can see by glancing at your level whether they're dealing with a newbie who might *need* help or a grizzled veteran who might *provide* help.

These same experience points are also what you use to upgrade your skills. Acquire 1000 XP for croaking a difficult monster, for example, and you can add those points to your archery skill to make yourself a more accurate shot. Over time, you're able to grow yourself into someone more formidable than the pipsqueak you start out as.

But the number of points required to upgrade skills increases as your character grows, and that means you have to put in more effort each time to improve your abilities. Many people see this creeping XP inflation as a perfect addiction system. XP begins to look like a drug after a while. You need more of it each time to get the same effect. So, you have to go after bigger and more difficult challenges every day. And this sense of growing challenge and competence is the common experience of all MMORPG players whether they're forming a guild, defending themselves from other players, selling items in the game economy, or joining a quest.

Failsafe

The ability to take big risks without ever having to suffer big punishments is, by far, the most striking feature of MMORPG cultures everywhere. It influences all of the other aspects of MMORPG life: quests, guilds, the economy, player killing, everything. And it's really what distinguishes the MMORPG universe from both the physical universe and from video games.

In a MMORPG you can commit any action you like without losing most of the points you've already piled up. The challenges that have to be met to acquire more points become more difficult over time. But the chances of a serious setback that takes away most of your hard-won XP are nil.

Essentially, what this means is that you can move forward every day in a MMORPG, and *never fall back* because the skills, talents, strengths, and expertise that you acquire on your travels can never be taken away from you. Even if you cheat or kill other people, you'll still prosper. Even if you devote yourself to your friends and throw yourself into spider-infested caves to save them, you'll still flourish. You can be as impulsive, destructive, or self-sacrificing as you like and you won't find yourself set back to zero, relegated to prison, or permanently dead. So, you're free to act in any way you choose.

In an ordinary video game your character passes through the world unchanged. You scroll across the landscape and travel to different levels in the game world, but, when you've vanquished the last boss, your character is still the same frenetic little hopper it was on the day you started.

In a MMORPG, by contrast, you change as you progress through life. This is possible because MMORPGs are persistent state universes. Like the real world, they continue to exist whether players are in them or not. Characters who log out of a world simply enter a state of suspended animation and reappear in the same place again when they log back in. No one freezes "his game" into a save state when they depart, the way they do with a traditional video game. So MMORPG characters can live and grow indefinitely. They become stronger, smarter, and more adept over time. And after they've piled up some experience, they're able to do things that they couldn't do when they started.

What really distinguishes MMORPG society from that of the real world, however, is not just that MMORPG characters grow. After all, people grow and improve themselves in the real world. What distinguishes MMORPG life is that once someone has improved, there's no way they can deteriorate. And it's this lack of any chance for downward mobility that sets the tone for all of MMORPG culture.

In real life, you can be the high-flying CEO of a multinational corporation one day and under indictment for fraud the next. You can be a self-indulgent rock diva cheered by millions in January and dragging yourself out of rehab in February. You can be president of the United States one morning and fleeing the White House under threat of impeachment that afternoon. But in the MMORPG realm, you cannot suffer this kind of catastrophic reversal of fortune. Once you've risen to a certain level, you cannot seriously decline. One bad decision cannot send your life spiraling into the pit as it can in the real world.

You can't even be felled by the ordinary savagery of life. You cannot become enfeebled by old age, hobbled by disease or accident, made obsolete by new technology, disabled, or permanently killed. If you acquire a particular skill, it's yours forever. And the more time you put into the world, the more skills you acquire. So, MMORPG worlds feature the attractive aspects of the real world without the risks of ultimate failure.

This makes virtual lands far more forgiving places than the real world. It instills in players a kind of confident optimism when facing the future that doesn't always exist in real life where bad decisions can be severely punished and bad luck can be merciless. And it is one significant reason that MMORPG players commit themselves to their characters in such a determined way. Often living with their avatars every day for years, players can rest assured that all of their hard work will not be undone by cruel circumstance. They can feel a kind of joy in daily irreversible progress that may be hard to come by in real life. And the sense of growth, improvement, and accomplishment — along with the assurance that they can't permanently lose any of the talents they've already acquired — serves to define MMORPG players and their culture as ultimately self-assured, optimistic, forward-looking, and even joyful.

Quests: Frodo, Take This Ring to Mordor

Quests — one of the basic components of MMORPG culture — work according to the all-carrot-no-stick principle that infuses every experience in the MMORPG world. They allow players to feel the joy and excitement of exploration without experiencing the hazards inherent in a real journey. Players on a MMORPG quest always feel *im*pelled to finish the quest because they get rewarded if they succeed, but rarely feel *com*pelled to finish because there is seldom any serious punishment for failure. And this system twists what would be dangerous, terror-filled journeys in the real world into exciting expeditions in the MMORPG realm.

Quests — also called missions or trials — are tasks that usually start with a rumor (a set of explanations, instructions, assignments, or requests) from an NPC called a rumormonger. In fantasy worlds, this is often a character who waits inside a hut in the woods and calls out to adventurers who stroll by. But in some games, mongers take the form of special monsters, Easter Island-style statue heads, or vending machines located in cities or space stations.

The most common form of mission is known as a fetch quest, FedEx quest, or mail run. In it, the player is asked to travel to a distant venue, convey a letter of introduction to another person, collect an object, or get a certificate stamped with a special seal, and then to return to the sender with proof of the accomplishment. The player then receives XP, money, a title, or a collectable whose value is related to the difficulty of the quest.

Sometimes the mission is multipart and becomes increasingly complex the further into it the player goes. A player may, for example, have to journey to a dungeon and fight the Ant Women (who squirt him with scent and drop a key), then unlock the treasure chest, obtain the relic bones, and return them to the hermit who checks for the ant scent while converting the relics into a powder which is sprinkled around a tree that produces a seed that grows into a vine that yields a poisonous fruit that is fed to a gelatinous wraith who offers a ring that protects the wearer from acid.

For some people, the bizarre complexity of such elaborate quests is part of their allure, while others are drawn to the camaraderie that's forced on players who are on an expedition together and are relying on each other for protection and support.

Not all quests are complex, however. Some of the quests that players spend their game lives completing are so simple and straightforward that they can be finished in an hour.

Slaughter quests, for example, require players to simply eliminate a specified number of creatures ("Kill 7 Bruxing Gnashers and bring me their incisors").

Scavenger hunts require players to gather a series of different objects from around the game world (eggs, pelts, feathers, jewels, musical instruments).

And treasure quests require players to overcome obstacles in order to retrieve valuable booty from remote and difficult locations.

But riddle quests are slightly more involved and complicated.

In a riddle quest, you may be presented with a couplet that makes sense only within the context of the game ("Where krakens twist and serpents gyre, there you'll find the Sacred Pyre"). Or you may be presented with a riddle and several choices:

"The certain knot of peace, the balm of woe, the poor man's wealth, the prisoner's release. What am I? Choices: Money, Science, or Sleep."

(According to Sir Walter Raleigh, the author of the verse, the answer is "sleep.")

A riddle may also be in graphical form. You may be presented, for example, with a collection of boxes color-coded to indicate their various strengths, and you may have to stack them in the order of the visible light spectrum to ascend to a ledge where a ticking bomb awaits.

Marathons, sometimes called orienteering quests, are an even more complicated form of quest — including intricate maps and complex travel instructions that lead players all over the virtual world in search of treasure and experience.

Lore quests, by contrast, are tied directly to the underlying plot of the game. They allow players to influence the storyline of the world they inhabit. Players may learn the lore of the world by completing the quest. Each time they finish a mission, for example, they may receive a little more information on the history and current affairs of the land. Or they may receive items that are referred to in the latest installment of lore. Or they may actually have a hand in creating the world's lore through their actions. (Their success or failure in finding an artifact or defeating a foe may become part of the game's official history.)

Title quests are similar, but they deal with personal history rather than world history. They are designed to grant a character an official honorific that becomes the prefix or suffix of his name. No one will ever address a character as "First Lieutenant Dandelion, Defender of the Meek, Slaughterer of the Necronomial Menace, Chancellor of the Exchequer, and Lord of All He Surveys," but some people collect such titles — the more ornate the better. And for many players, these kinds of quests are the richest part of the game experience.

Almost all MMORPG players take part in quests at one time or another. And players have different reasons for entering quests and for finding them compelling. A Minnesota administrative assistant in her early 50s, for example, whose youngest child had just gone off to college leaving her with some time on her hands, explained her love of quests by saying that she didn't want her real life to be "exciting." Some of her friends had had exciting lives full of vicious divorces, alcohol problems, job layoffs, breast cancer, and bankruptcy. In real life, she said, "exciting" was always "bad." When something exciting happened to you, you ended up talking to lawyers, doctors, creditors, and psychiatrists — the four horsemen of the personal apocalypse. So she didn't want excitement in her real life. But she didn't want to fall asleep either. So quests were a good compromise. She could feel invigorated and enthused while pursuing the quests. But she didn't have to go to the hospital afterward.

Another player, living in the mountains of Colorado in real life, said that he regarded missions as a family bonding activity. He explained that his family had three separate accounts on the same game, three computers in their home, and a router so they (father, mother, and eight-year-old son) could all sign on at the same time and play together. It was their "family time," especially in the winter when the snow was too deep to play outside. And they often created their own personal quests when the packaged ones didn't entice them.

In fact, many players build player quests that are similar to the game engine's missions involving traveling to another part of the world and accomplishing a particular feat, but which also include a humorous component as well, with fluorescent pink armor or vases of wilted sunflowers serving as the prizes.

When asked what they liked about all of the different forms of quest, players answered in a multitude of ways. Some said loot was the important factor for them. All of the best trophy items were at the end of the quests, so greed was their motivating factor. Other players said that quests inserted them into the ongoing narrative. It was as if questing players were allowed inside one chapter of the "game book" during the mission. Instead of reading about someone else's adventures, players could experience them firsthand. The quest, in a sense, erased the line between myth and reality. An equal number said the quest gave them a specific purpose in interacting with people and creatures in the game world. It clarified their goals in life. And many people also said that the best part of questing was the sense of mateship that was forced on players by the difficulty of the task. When quests were too hard to handle alone, questers ended up making friends with other players on the road, players they might never have met otherwise. And this was a great plus for them.

Almost everyone mentioned, in one way or another, the fact that quests represented excitement and purpose in their lives without the risk of actual physical danger. People on a quest could be immersed in and mesmerized by an exciting task in the same way that they were mesmerized by a thriller movie. But they could also participate in what was exciting them. They could feel their hearts pound and their pulses quicken. And they could leap off cliffs, charge into crowds of armed villains, and rush into dangerous caverns to save their friends — all the while knowing that there would be no physical consequences for failing. Their characters might be killed, and that would certainly be inconvenient. But there was no way that the players themselves could suffer in any way as a result of bad luck or bad decisions. And this was intensely attractive to many players.

Guilds: The Three Thousand Musketeers

Another feature that helps define MMORPG society is the concept of the guild or player association, a feature that often provides the scaffolding for a game world's social structure and becomes a major part of a MMORPG player's life. (For some players, in fact, guild life is so much more rewarding than real life that it's embraced in a way that real-world social interactions are never embraced.) And the guild system works in the same way that the quest system works. It allows players to enjoy all the benefits of something — in this case, a social life — without any of the drawbacks.

One player I spoke with in a guild mansion, for example, admitted freely to a sentiment voiced by many other players. He said his guild colleagues were better than his real family. He had friends he could count on and connect with in the game world, but they weren't like relatives. He didn't hang around with his game world friends because he was stuck with them genetically. He associated with them because he cherished their friendship (and could simply walk away from them if they became disagreeable).

This sense of meaningful relationships without the pain of maintenance is a very common sentiment among guild members, and one of the defining aspects of all-carrot-no-stick MMORPG culture.

Guilds are organizations created by the players themselves to assist other players inside the game. Sometimes called allegiance groups, tribes, factions, societies, or clans, the purposes of guilds run the gamut of human attitude and endeavor. Some are peaceful mutual aid societies. Others are profit-making corporations. Some are quasireligious groups with their own law and lore. Others are violent virtual biker gangs. And there are even guilds that act as "mafia dating services" arranging violent trysts for characters who want to gang up in order to make an assault on another clan or kill some despised opponent.

A common model for an allegiance group is the medieval craftsmen's guild. Organizations with names like the League of Benevolence, All for One, and The Society of the Common Weal organize themselves in a way that allows high-level master players to work with journeymen, and journeymen to assist new apprentices in learning the ropes.

Another popular guild type is the cartel—a group open only to mercantile characters who spend their time buying components, arranging deals, and manufacturing and selling finished goods. These organizations, with names like Mine Not Yours, All for Me, Avarice Before Honor, and Everything Must Go, set the low prices that their members pay for raw materials and the high prices outsiders pay for the finished goods. They may help their members create automated bots to sell their products. Or they may even build shops or entire towns for guild participants to hawk their wares in.

When asked about the notion that guilds facilitate all the best aspects of social and economic life without any of the liabilities, one guild member, a Chicago software engineer in real life, added a comment on the politics of the virtual world that many other players agreed with. He said that guilds were a kind of "communism" done right. This, surprisingly, turns out to be quite a common view among guild members.

One character alone, he explained, could spend a year collecting all of the components needed to assemble a complex device. But a guild could ask its members to fan out in small groups and collect all of the necessary components in one day. Complex items beyond the reach of any individual player could then be quickly constructed by the guild and loaned to everyone. The guild could also accept donations from members and then distribute those contributions to others according to their needs. Everyone benefited as a result. There were always some slackers and parasites, he said. But, over all, the system worked. Guild life made game life less burdensome in the same way that a supportive family made real life less burdensome.

Another ardent guild proponent, a Missouri landscaper in real life, confessed that his membership in the guild made him feel needed. His apprentices needed advice and assistance from him every day, and he delighted in giving it.

When asked if he couldn't find the same sense of fulfillment in real life, he said guild life was nothing like real life. People weren't afraid to help each other in the guild. He could be nice to people in the game world and not worry about being taken advantage of or getting sued.

Another player, a marketer in Baltimore, joined his guild as a point of honor. He said that so many guild people had helped him when he'd first entered the game that he felt as if he had to return the favor. He said he was "completing the circle" by joining the guild and being generous to its members.

For some players guild life is obviously the adhesive that sticks their eyes to the screen for months at a time, so it's a fundamental component of MMORPG culture. People who are natural organizers love running a virtual organization. And those who are naturally gregarious love the social interplay and persiflage. In fact, these things thrill them enough that many players happily abandon "inferior" real-world social interaction to get what they crave in the game.

A business consultant in California said that he preferred the people in his guild to the people in his real life and that he wouldn't want to go through the day without meeting up with his MMORPG companions. They offered him something that he couldn't get in real life — the chance to mingle with friends when he craved friendship, and the chance to ignore them completely when he wanted solitude. He could be sociable when he was in the mood and curmudgeonly at will. He could have all the benefits of an active social life without the burdensome entanglements and obligations. And that was a big reason why he preferred MMORPG life to real life.

Game Economies: Greed as a Creed

This idea of living a life without negative consequences leads to two kinds of player behavior in MMORPGs: heroic altruism on the one hand and sneaky villainy on the other. Some players feel free to become philanthropic for the first time in their lives without the gnawing worry of getting hurt themselves as they help other people. But others suddenly feel free to hurt other people because they know they won't be punished for it. And, sadly, the number of these latter types is quite large in most MMORPG worlds. Vile players see MMORPGs as the place where they can take advantage of others without paying the price for bad behavior, so the dark side of MMORPG culture is shaped by these players.

Villainous players concentrate their efforts in two areas — war and commerce. And for many of them, the two are interchangeable. For some strange reason, game economies act as magnets for people whose instincts run toward the greedy, vicious, deceitful, and self-aggrandizing. And mean and duplicitous behavior are part of every MMORPG's culture because people can lie, swindle, bilk, defraud, bamboozle, and steal from each other in the game world without any of the penalties such behavior would garner in the real world.

Many characters, in fact, spend their game lives engaged in economic pursuits that they regard as battles. A deal, to these players, is not just an exchange of goods for money. It's a military skirmish with winners and losers. And trouncing other players in financial matters is something they delight in.

These mercantile-warrior players display certain obvious behaviors.

Their competitive bragging, for example, often takes the shape of a higher level character stealing a lower level's kill and then bending down to loot the creature's corpse while boasting that he has just found the rarest treasure in the game on this particular body.

This happens so often in some games that many of the declarations of "Woot! Phat loot! You missed it!" are surely fabricated. And it suggests that the urge to flaunt superiority is so strong in some folks that they'll even lie to do it. Because they want to lord it over the suckers and losers around them, they'll pretend that the creature corpses they just stole from other players are loaded with expensive goods — even if the corpses actually contain nothing but fish pies and old socks.

This same type of behavior — designed to both impress and antagonize other characters — also occurs at merchant shops where a player choosing new armor from among a collection of loot just deposited by other players will announce, "Whoa! Who just dropped off this level 300 breastplate that I'm scooping up! Whoa man! You only see this stuff once in a lifetime!"

The purpose behind such pronouncements seems to be to let other players know that they're missing out on something big or that they're far less adept than the character celebrating his own clever shrewdness.

A behavior in the same vein occurs when a business character tries to bully, cajole, browbeat, or trick another character into consummating a deal.

A player interviewed in one game, for example, had four bags of diamond powder to sell and was told by trustworthy friends that they could be exchanged for 14 notes each. He offered his goods for sale in the town square where people stood around calling out what they had to sell, and, after only a minute, another character sent a "/tell" (private message) claiming that diamond powders were only worth one note each. The deceiving player said this in a tone that suggested he was a knowledgeable friend whispering to a naïve younger player. He then offered to buy all the player's diamond powders for one note each.

Another character then approached and said he'd pay nine notes for each one. But, when the trade was completed, it turned out that he had placed only seven notes on the trading block for each powder. He then immediately turned around and publicly announced that he was selling for 14 notes each the very diamond powders he had just bought — in capital letters no less — in order to emphasize his business triumph and prove that he had bested someone in a deal and screwed them out of their profit.

This kind of very common behavior represents the bleaker side of MMORPG culture. And it turns some players into cynics, souring them on the whole notion of generosity in the MMORPG world. A fascinating conversation overheard in a hinterlands dungeon, for example, perfectly illustrated the opposing views of proper game behavior that players come up with after dealing with other MMORPG inhabitants.

One player cried out that he needed a healing kit for his wounds. Someone offered him several kits for free, but a third player jumped in to prevent the exchange, screaming that no one should just give things away because people weren't worth it.

The player offering the kits said he had more than enough and he knew what it was like to be in need. But the cynical player blasted him and tried to block the act of altruism by dragging monsters into the vicinity to kill everyone in the dungeon.

It was a snapshot of both MMORPG and real-world society. On the one hand was a character defending the notion that people are generally evil and anxious to take advantage of compassionate suckers and do-gooders. On the other hand was a character representing the view that anyone's life can be overtaken by catastrophe and that helping people when they're down is the natural response of anyone who has been down himself.

Sadly, many MMORPG players eventually come to take a dim view of their fellow players because they're abused so often. In interviews, a huge number of players admitted that they had been shortchanged, cheated, or taken advantage of by other players. In fact, more than half of them said this was a regular occurrence in their game lives. It was not something most people would have guessed when they first entered the game world, but, as it turned out, the most villainous aspects of real life were amplified by the all-carrot-no-stick culture of MMORPGs.

To see for myself how money was regarded in MMORPG society, I conducted a series of fiscal experiments in the game world. And the results confirmed the experiences of the other players around me.

First, I took a full set of my best armor off one of my mules along with some Crystal Swords. I then proceeded to a newbie town, resolved that the first person who acted honestly toward me would receive all the equipment and millions of coins for free. All he had to do was pass a simple test.

I gave each person a Crystal Sword. Then I announced, "Oh, wait. If you give me that sword back, I'll give you another one that's even better."

Crystal Swords are twice the size of ordinary swords and look so impressive that newbies find them irresistible. I knew that. But I wanted to see who would give the sword back. No one did.

The first person said nothing, kept the sword, and waited for me to leave. I explained again, and he handed me an old wooden club that had been cluttering up one of his packs. "Here. Take this," he said.

This same scenario repeated itself three more times with three other people. Even though these folks knew that I was obviously a good-natured and generous person, they were all still ready to cheat me out of the sword, even when they were promised a better one in return.

Another time I decided to give all my money away — also with disastrous results.

It takes lower level players many weeks of play to save up one note's worth of money, so I went around dropping notes on newbies and lowbies to see what would happen.

Of 20 players who received my largesse, 11 never even said thank you. They simply ran away with the money. Another five typed "thx" or "ty" and scampered off. And one was made so furious by the unexpected munificence that he tracked me down, shot lightning bolts at my face, and threw the money back at me, storming off in protest.

Only three people stopped to say thank you. Two of them offered items in return. And one said he'd been killed so many times in the desert that he was now broke, bloodied, and armorless. He had been picking up apples in the fields to sell for equipment. For him the note translated into 200 fewer hours of tedious apple-picking, and he thanked me profusely. That made up for the other 19 responses. But the fact that so many people had simply run off with the money was a little disconcerting. It was like living one of Mother Theresa's exhortations: You may find that people take advantage of you when you're generous. Be generous anyway.

Even more frightening than the culture of belligerent greed, however, is the culture of player killing that's based on the same commit-any-action-without-consequences idea as all the other uniquely MMORPG cultural efflorescences. In this case, however, it translates into murder without imprisonment.

Killer Be Killed

Games that allow players to kill each other (called PvP — player versus player — or PK — player-killer — games) have led to the development of a separate subculture in the MMORPG universe — a violent, creepy, ornery, impatient, petulant subculture, and one with a very different set of rules from the usual PvE (Player versus Environment) MMORPG game. It's a subculture that draws certain players into the virtual world and keeps them there because it guarantees them the chance to commit acts of the most extreme violence without repercussions. In fact, the dominant aspect of this culture is to see the slaughtering of other human beings as both a lifestyle choice and a sport in the manner of Roman gladiatorial contests.

When you first enter PK worlds, they seem to be the hap-happiest places around. There's a lot of high-fiving, rejoicing, and dancing. On closer inspection, though, you discern that what passes for merriment is really either vicious mockery and the vilification of enemies or celebration after the killing of other human beings. The atmosphere is festive all right, but only when the enemies' internal organs are being roasted like marshmallows on sticks over campfires.

The PK culture revolves around clan wars, gang rivalries, vengeance quests, blood feuds, and bounty hunting. Some PK games even weave into their game engine features that add to the murderous and bloodthirsty texture of the game.

Shrunken head quests, for example, in which the goal is to kill a player in another tribe and turn in his head or helmet for a prize, are part of some games. Race wars are part of most PK games, awarding bonus points for killing someone of an enemy race. Property destruction may be part of the game as well, guaranteeing that some characters will make enemies by laying siege to towns, smashing castle walls, and razing villages. In fact, territorial disputes may be built into the fiber of the game by allowing characters to claim real estate gained through the conquest of other players.

All of these factors fundamentally change how PKers see virtual life and how it should be lived. In fact, PK worlds — unlike most MMORPG worlds — would fit anyone's definition of fascist societies. In them, all other players are differentiated as either allies or enemies. A state of emergency and martial law always exists. The military (the loot getters), the business community (the loot processors), and the government (the loot administrators) are very closely allied. The press (in the form of forums and chats) is controlled by Guild Monitors and features chanting and sloganeering rather than reasoned dialogue. "Fear and anger" are renamed "vigilance and justice" and are promoted as virtues. Opinions outside the guild's party line are denounced as cowardice or treason. And the animosity that soaks the landscape prevents players from traveling beyond their little home regions, so they never experience a different interpretation of game life.

In most PK games, players band together into clans for mutual protection, vengeance, control of territory, and the persecution of enemies. With names like Shallow Grave, The Undertakers, The Overtakers, and Apocalyptic Nightmare, PK guilds take on the characteristics of both bellicose nation-states and warring Cosa Nostra families. They pay bounties for the slaughter of marked enemies, hold grisly ceremonies to honor their "made men," organize their new members into hit squads, and wage war on other tribes for the control of resources and land.

Some players keep records of every duel they participate in, and these individual records sometimes grow into revenge databases — living documents tracing the history of contention between the clans.

Particularly destructive players may even take out contracts on other players. These are posted on kill-this-bastard bulletin boards around the Internet. In fact, entire guilds may pay mercenaries to kill their enemies or they may assign their younger members to bounty quests in which the goal is to gank the enemy (a PK term — a contraction of "gang up on and kill" — that suggests surprising the opponent with many more attackers than he can defend against). Successful gankers get uber-booty and titles conveyed by the guild leadership.

All of this means that player-killers — called red dots in many games because they show up on radar as red dots whereas other players show up as green or blue dots — are a different breed. And games with 100% of their land set aside for player killing have a different ethos than other MMORPG games. They have a different feel to them, a different smell (the smell of napalm in the morning, perhaps). And the emotional environment is quite striking to anyone used to a normal MMORPG game.

In a non–PK MMORPG (or in a game that allows player killing in only a few areas of its landscape) the aura is mostly one of perseverance, striving toward a goal, perpetual improvement, and camaraderie. In a fully PK world, however, the emotional tone is one of constant petulance, back-stabbing, wariness, taunting, ambushes, paranoia, vulgarity, order-giving, order-following, endocrine spurts, mood swings, wild anger, willfulness, and declarations of hatred. PKers may describe their lives as filled with glorious battles, heroic escapades, the thrill of the hunt, and united defense against villainous attacks. But a few months in any purely PK game would disabuse new players of that romantic view of PK life.

How did this culture start? Player killing began as a way to mix the dynamics of FPS (first-person shooter) games like Quake and Doom into the MMORPG world. But when player killing entered the MMORPG realm, it transformed from a *mano a mano* exercise in strategy and stealth into large-scale warfare.

In most FPS games, every player is at the same level, and victory is mostly the result of clever planning, tactics, and surprise. In a PK MMORPG, however, each of the characters is at a different level of development, so powerful players and large groups are always favored. Players who get into the game just after its commercial release, especially players who are good at persuading other characters to join their alliance, become the big shots. And, after a few months, there is no way to catch up to them or defeat them without help from many other players. That pretty much eliminates the role of the lone gunslinger, trader, or explorer traveling from town to town in a fully PK game. And that makes the game less fun for the player who comes into it to be a wildcat, desperado, masterless samurai, or lone wolf.

This system also makes life as a younger character a different experience from life in a non–PK game. If you're a level five, for example, in a land full of level 50s (all of whom can squash you like a bug) you spend a lot of time kowtowing. The phrases "Yes, sir" and "No, sir" become part of your permanent vocabulary, and you utter them to characters you'd just as soon clutch by the throat and throttle into the dirt.

To an outsider entering this kind of world for a look around, the place looks like a realm of pettiness, childish vengeance cycles, ludicrous swaggering, silly first-grade shoving matches, and spiritual bankruptcy. And it is. But all of the intrigue and subterfuge, viciousness, political maneuvering, swooping blitzkriegs, bloody private duels, posturing, and bravado are what PKers live for.

Ask any group of regular PK players and they'll always mention the thrill of hunting other human beings. They'll talk about pounding hearts, flushed faces, screams of frustration, torrents of rage, and gushing fountains of adrenaline. They'll point out the satisfaction of revenge, the wild-eyed hysteria of free-for-all battles, the brinksmanship before a war, and the constant violent banter in the middle of a street fight. PK life is more spleen than brain, more knee-jerk reaction than thoughtful stratagem, more testosterone than neurotransmitter. But PKers find it more real, more visceral, more evocative of true ugly human nature than mere creature-based MMORPGs.

In fact, the most common comment by PKers about their lives is that PK life is "just like real life." According to this view, killing people and taking the loot from their corpses is obviously how anyone — a person, an organization, a country — becomes more powerful. And power is the only goal really worth striving for. The more people you kill, the more loot you acquire. The more people you kill, the greater your fearsome reputation becomes. The more people you kill, the more you can force your will on the living. Killing people and taking what they have is "natural." Helping people without a selfish motive, acting for the common good, indulging in artistic or spiritual pursuits, forgiving others, being generous, demonstrating altruism, and the whole notion of a civilized society being one in which the strong protect the weak makes no sense at all in this view. The role of the strong is obviously to crush the weak in the PK view. That's what logic dictates. Anything else would be contrary to human nature. And PK worlds make this logic manifest.

The player killing life is clearly not everyone's cup of tea (actually, PKers would say "cup of blood"). And PKers will probably never represent a majority of MMORPG gamers because most players don't want to go PK. In fact, some games ban the practice entirely. But, in the games where player killing is the dominant cultural factor, it's why many players enter the virtual world in the first place. If they couldn't battle and ambush other humans, what would be the point of playing?

And player killing, wherever it flourishes, is entirely representative of the essential element that defines all MMORPG cultures — the ability of players to experience the joys and triumphs of life without the physical risks and punishing failures. Players can grow without ever having to worry about old age, drunken drivers, or deadly pathogens taking away their accomplishments. They can associate with their friends whenever they like but can ignore them the rest of the time — without suffering any social stigma. They can go off on exciting quests without even considering travelers' diarrhea or terrorist attacks. They can screw their fellow players out of fortunes without interference from the police or the government. And they can kill at will without a thought about jail time.

In the all-carrot-no-stick world of MMORPG culture, every day offers another chance to do what you love without paying for the privilege. And that may be why people are drawn to MMORPGs in such huge numbers. Who wouldn't be attracted to such a place?

Chapter 3

The Psychology
of MMORPG Players

"Only real life is unfair."— Anonymous MMORPG player

"The future looks bleak for reality."— Anonymous MMORPG player

The MMORPG world presents players with choices that the real world doesn't. It allows players to choose a new outer form, for example, a new name for themselves, and a new way of interacting with the world around them. These kinds of choices made by players while they're in the game illustrate not only how players view their characters, but why they play in the MMORPG world and even how they see themselves in the real world. By looking at the choices players make in the creation of their characters, it's possible to learn something about how MMORPG players think and how they could be attracted to a virtual world in the first place.

A Dolorous Moonglum by Any Other Name

The easiest way to understand something about the thought processes of MMORPG players is to look at the names they choose for their characters. In one or two words, displayed for everyone in the world to see, players often reveal their deepest desires, most fervent interests, and true character. And the range and depth of names is quite surprising.

Gamers have the reputation, after all, of being vidiots, of spending all their time with games instead of books. But this is definitely not the case with MMORPG participants. Any new player can see that the other players are readers by just looking at the names players choose for their characters — a huge number of which are derived from fantasy novels.

One day of random sampling, in fact, turned up The Dragon Reborn from Robert Jordan's *Wheel of Time,* Sabriel from Garth Nix's novel of the same name, Shadowdancer from the Mercedes Lackey books, Ankh-Morpork from Terry Pratchett's Discworld series, Stainless Steel Rat from the Harry Harrison novels, Allanon from *The Sword of Shannara* by Terry Brooks, Firbolg from *Rhapsody* by Elizabeth Haydon, Bilbo Baggins from Tolkien's *The Hobbit,* Pug of Crydee from Raymond Feist's *Magician: Apprentice,* Muab Dib from Frank Herbert's *Dune,* Polgara The Sorceress from the David Eddings novels, Truthseeker from the *Sword Of Truth* series by Terry Goodkind, and Raistlin, Fistandantillus, and Huma Paladine from Weis and Hickman's *Dragonlance* series.

Many players with these names told me that they saw themselves as entering a book when they entered a MMORPG game. Some people even admitted that they had tried to fashion their own real lives after the lives of their favorite fictional characters, and that the game finally gave them the chance to create a separate identity with that goal in mind.

Others said that after a lifetime of reading about and imagining alternate worlds, the game became a way of finally seeing and traveling through those worlds. Game life, one character explained, allowed him to use his real eyes and ears instead of his mind's eye and ear.

A large number of people also choose historical or mythological figures for their character names, showing themselves to be widely read. In one week I discovered Tokugawa, Ptolemy, William Wallace, Sun Tzu, Octavius Augustus, both Grendel and Beowulf, Machiavelli, Valkyrie (the Nordic maidens who led dead warriors to Valhalla, the Viking heaven), Lethe (the River of Forgetfulness the ancient Greek dead crossed to forget about their past lives), Dainichi (sun god of the esoteric Shingon Buddhist sect), Phaedra (the betrayed woman in the Greek drama *Hippolitus* by Euripides), Arjuna (Krishna's charioteer in the

Bhagavad-gita), Cuchulain (the legendary Irish hero), Zhang He (the Chinese naval explorer), William Shakespeare (some English writer), Ashoka (the Indian warlord turned Buddhist king), Vlad Tzepesh, Dracool, The Impaler, Vlod Dracul, and Nosferatu (these last five all names for Dracula), Aeolus (the ancient Greek god of the wind), Hiawatha, The Hydra, Imhotep, Charon the Ferryman (conveyer of the dead across the river Styx), Fleh Cher Cris Chun (from *Mutiny on the Bounty*), Dar Tanyan (from *The Three Musketeers*), Deus Ex Machina (the Latin expression "god from a machine" which describes a divine character in Roman theater lowered onto the stage with a pulley to solve the play's plot problems and rescue the hero), and both Scylla and Charybdis.

These people were an educated lot. Among their names were classical references, historical allusions, and obscure mythological arcana that no zombified thumb-twitcher would ever have known. Just by asking people about their names one could see that a lot of MMORPG players were scholarly, even erudite, not at all what a nongamer would expect.

Other players were more subtle with their names, even devious. And their monikers demonstrated a philological temperament. Some of them were quite clever, in fact. In one world were Philogynist, Bakasama ("Mister Dummy" in Japanese), Hukt Awn Fonix, X. Perry Mental, Ali Gory, Ms. Aree, Jokrzwylde, Ichorous (a pun on both arrogance and gore), VI Miniac, Miss Anne Thropy, Kharma Sucra (created by a pastry chef interested in the 100 ways to prepare a torte), Hg (the periodic table symbol for Mercury, created by a chemist with both a fast character and an interest in mythology), and Anubiz (created by an entrepreneur with an interest in Egyptology who had just started a new business).

The most lilting names came from players who were poets at heart, players who took a delight in language. They were often voracious readers but also had a creative streak that made them want to, in a sense, write their own two-word novels, rather than just replicate what other people had written. In one forest full of poets lurked Fatal Solitude, Oaken Heart, Pinioned Angel, Red Scorpion, Zulu Dawn, Ashen Light, Poison Arrow Frog, Ash Forest, Veiled Shadow, Translucent Ember, Emerald Sun, Rosemary Thyme (This was actually a husband-and-wife team playing one character. Their other character was The Parsley Sage.),

Ice Queen, King Bee, Evening Enchantress, Angel Goddess, Christmas Presents, Seawind Oceanus, Dolorous Moonglum, Ebony Steelbreeze, Aurora Australis, Desert Rose, Calm B IV The Storm, Lion Claw, Burning Hierophant, Linear Mist, Night Wind, and Midnight Falcon.

And there were also plenty of comical names and names with meanings only their creators understood, names like Boney Jellyfish, Yuri Sonovobich, Sideshow Cereal Bowl, Flash A'aa, Universal Remote, Dizzium, Hal Itosis, Mad Cow, Cookie Thief, Fungus of Light, Beastfang Lumberjack, Unleashed Newt, Limping Ox, Mullet God, Urine Luck, Camel Toe, Pink Squirrel, Tatoochick, Thundergod of Cheese, Chocolate Weasel, Major Flatulence, Nochi Ryu (which turned out to be the English word "no," the Chinese word "chi," and the Japanese word "ryu" conjoined to signify "no power dragon"), Mr. Oysterhead, Eye Vannah, Badabing Badaboom, Krum Cookiecutter, Red the Odoriferous, Wonko the Plinker, Meglo the Maniac, Ravenous Spacechicken, Latex Toad, Red Hot Bessy, Ronnie the Evil One, Bad Beth, and Risqué (a character created by a French female player who regularly doffed her armor and paraded around town in her undies).

There was even a middle-brow level of players — those who had plucked their names from the other broadly defined branches of fantasy media, including Kozure Okami (from the Japanese manga, *Lone Wolf And Cub*), Disciple of Grace (from the Magic: The Gathering cards), Enzo (from the 3D animated series *Reboot*), Protos (from the video game *Starcraft*), Freak the Mighty (from the young adult novel by the Philbricks), Green Lantern (from the comic books), Arashikage (Storm Shadow from the GI Joe action figures), Art Vandelay (from Seinfeld), Pray for Mojo (from The Simpsons), Moose Wants a Cookie (from the kids' books by Laura Numeroff), Borg Collective (a Star Trek reference used by programmers as a slang designation for Microsoft), Moriarty (from the Sherlock Holmes mysteries), Never Winter Knight (from the game *NeverWinter Nights*), NeopetLover (a reference to the kids' Web game), Furby Eater (a reference to the toy), Jigglypuff (from the Pokemon cards), and Disco Barbie.

Most interesting were the names of characters whose players recognized the hold the game had on them, characters with names like Obsessed, Obsessive, Addictive, Addicted, Bitten, Trapped, Compulsive, and Needa Life.

Sometimes players used their names to identify themselves as members of a particular group. French folks on one server, for example, all chose Gallic names ending in "ix" harkening back to Vercingetorix (who confronted Caesar in 52 B.C.) and Asterix (the wily French comic book hero). Many Australians chose identifying names as well: Vege-Might, WizardOfOz, Corroboree, and Gday M8. And, for unfathomable reasons, the Danish contingent all gave themselves the title "Crazy"— Crazy Charlie, Crazy Mary, Crazy Turtle, Crazy Bow, Crazy Oracle, Crazy Snake, Crazy Julia. Whenever I met a Crazy person I knew to say "Hej! Jebii!"

Some players intentionally restricted their choice of name to fit in with a band of friends. One such group, for example, was the Cheese Clan, all of whose members were named after cheese. Whole real-world families were part of the clan, all sporting similar names: Easy Mac-nCheese, Cheddar Garbo, Feta Garbo, Brie Z, Jane Fondue, Head Cheese, Hu Cut the Cheez, Velveta Elvis (a reference to the cheesy Velvet Elvis paintings sold at flea markets), and Gouda Betta Best. The strangest aspect of the group was that no one could tell me why they had started using cheese references in the first place.

Many other players, excited by the violence of the MMORPG world, made that violence part of their identity. And their names took on a dark and foreboding cast: Dark Templar, Dark Cloud, Dark Clown, Dark Angel, Dark Temptress, Dark Dude, Dark Incantation, Dark Light, DOA, Shootchu, Maximum Evil, Death Prophet, Hellbound, Hellborn, Hell Monkey, Cowboy from Hell, Nightmare, Daymare, Morbid Isolation, Righteous Indignation, Evisceration, Lamentation, La Malediction, Smirking Revenge, Demonic Esper, Blood King, Oblivion, Maniac of Death, Drips with Venom, Night of Apocalypse, End Time, Ikillyoudead, Small Poxx, Large Poxx, Bonebreaker, Raging Coffin Dancer, Mean Guy, Abra-Cadaver (a war mage), Cry Havoc, Buckets of Blood, Tazer, Pepper Spray, Toksik, Sayten, Nekromanser, Dyre Konsikuences, Inrage, Malen'Colley, Sleyr, Jak da Reaper, Chemical Imbalance, Bounte Hunter, and Slacthaus ("Slaughterhouse" in German).

The only players who would probably be legally pursued because of their names, however, were those who had chosen corporate monikers. Just one afternoon's jaunt through the game landscape revealed FedEx

Man, Mayor McCheese, Pillsbury Toeboy, Captain Crunch, Killing for Dummies, Liquid Plumber, Magi Kingdom, Orkin Man, Staples, Starbucks, and Rogue Jedi. With all this borrowing from corporate culture, it's only a matter of time before trademark lawyers invade the virtual world with cease and desist notices for players who are "illegally expropriating corporate intellectual property." As for myself, I chose Sugar Glider (a squirrel-like marsupial in Australia that dodges predators by leaping and gliding from tree to tree, and lives more by luck than intelligence). And it's a name I've used in all the MMORPGs I've played, so I'm generally happy with it. But its one big drawback is that everyone tends to contract it to "Sugar," which makes it sound like an endearment.

There I am withstanding a withering bludgeoning from an uber-level metal-clad ox-gelder monster while hurling mighty flame blasts at the villainous titans surrounding me, and someone calls over, "Need any help, Sugar?" as if I'm sipping mint julips on the veranda with a whist-playing contingent of southern ladies. I hear the name and think, "How y'all doing, Sugar? Can I get you some more tea, Sugar? Why don't y'all come over here and give me some sugar, Sugar."

This is hardly the desired linguistic connotation for a feared and mighty warrior. So, in the future I may append some token of my glorious fearsomeness to the name, just to make it a little more intimidating. Baleful Sugar Glider of Death, maybe. Or Evil Blood-Soaked Sugar Glider from Hell.

In general, an investigation of the many thousands of names in MMORPG worlds shows, first, that players transfer the interests of their real lives into their virtual lives and, second, that MMORPG players are far more self-reflective, clever, literate, and thoughtful than nongamers might think.

A large number of names fall under the rubric of mystical because every game's landscape is otherworldly, and people interested in lyricism and mysticism are drawn to such places. Some of the names are obviously morbid because some players enter the world specifically to commit violent and deadly acts. But there are plenty of mellifluous names as well, maybe because life in the virtual world is often a dreamy affair, especially when gazing down from a cliff onto the sweeping plains at sunset or when first breaking into a secret subterranean passage and discovering untrodden crystalline caverns below.

All of these separate elements — the fantasy, the pugnacity, the lyricism, and the literary streak among the players — shows up in game after game. So, they are clearly part of the worldview of the players. They demonstrate that MMORPG participants have retained a sense of enchantment in their lives, a sense that, even in a vile and banal real world, heroic quests, intrigue, mystery, and exploration are still possible in life. And they reveal that many MMORPG players are thoughtful, even spiritual, intellectuals rather than bullet-headed drones.

Reality Is Only Skin Deep

For the last 20 years, virtual reality researchers have been pondering one question: Will people who have the chance to create a second life from scratch choose virtual selves identical to their real selves or will they opt for disguises? In the MMORPG world that question can finally be answered.

The expectation had always been that most people were not happy with their physical appearance and would, therefore, create a brand new body if they were given the chance. Older people would create spry young avatars with flowing tresses. Men would create shapely female personas. Women would adopt broad-shouldered don't-mess-with-me male facades. Kids would design overgrown mesomorphs. And no one would be unimaginative enough to actually construct a replacement self that looked just like his real self.

The thought was that people would shed any physical trait that smacked of weakness. Obesity, small stature, baldness, gray hair, childhood, any form of physical infirmity — even the female gender in some situations — would be cast off. Anything that could be derided in a shallow money-size-power-and-good-looks culture would be tossed aside. Everyone in the virtual world would be 25 years old, male, six feet five inches tall, rippling with muscles, in perfect health, and Hollywood gorgeous.

The truth of character creation, however, turns out to be quite different from the expectations. And it reveals a great deal about the psychology of MMORPG players.

In cases where players have only human races to work with, a huge number of MMORPG players who are younger than 15 and older than 40 choose avatars that are astoundingly similar to their real selves. Players at these two ends of the age spectrum tend to create characters with the same gender, hair color, physical features, complexion, and body plan as their real selves. But players who are between those ages experiment wildly with physiognomy, gender, height, and every other physical characteristic.

The reason this is interesting is that, in many games, a character's abilities depend on skill and experience, not appearance. So, things like haircut and gender don't matter. In these games players can choose any features they want without compromising their abilities. And yet a sizeable number of older and very young players consistently choose to apply their own actual appearances to their virtual selves.

Why is this? Well, identifying with the character seems to depend on the stage of life that the human being behind the character is experiencing. Children choose to recreate their real appearances perhaps because they are less self-conscious, more contented with themselves, or too self-absorbed to consider deviating from their own real physiognomy. And people over 40 may have become so comfortable with themselves or so accustomed to seeing a certain face in the mirror every morning that they build their new selves to reflect that ingrained sense of identity.

Older women players in the MMORPG world often experiment with hair color —flaming red seems to be the popular choice over gray — but, among males, the graybeards in real life become graybeards in the virtual world too, the bald guys become bald guys, and the snow-on-the-roof-fire-in-the-furnace crowd sport their ivory locks in game worlds everywhere. Some of them will tell you that their white hair is a badge of accomplishment. But most seem to treat it as a kind of armor against condescension. White hair is a way of telling other players, "Don't try to hose me, junior. I've been around the block."

Creating an identical virtual self actually enhances the verisimilitude of the game for these players. The character becomes part of the player's self, rather than something outside of it. Choosing a nine-foot-tall, blue-green, muscle-bound amphibian as an avatar would make the game less real than choosing a character that looks like the player's true self. With the amphibian, it isn't really the player in the game defeating the monsters and overcoming the obstacles. It's just some cartoon character. A character that looks like the player is easier to imbue with the person's own ego and personality.

The majority of players, however — those who do *not* create replicas of their real selves — prefer to hide their real identities behind avatars that are completely different in size, shape, gender, and appearance. These players often regard disguising their real selves as part of the game experience. They see their disguise as an integral part of their play strategy. And choosing a different appearance becomes a calculated ploy used to intimidate others, avoid problems, remain incognito, or gain an advantage.

Switching genders is the most popular way to do this, and it's actually a strategic decision. Male players who create female characters in a MMORPG very often report that female characters are given things in the game by male characters — good armor, better weapons, money, and more powerful spells. Instead of flowers and a meal, they are given axes and helmets in a kind of primitive courtship ritual. And many players want to take advantage of this innate mating impulse in their fellow players.

Others have discovered that Player Killers are more inclined to have mercy on a female character — even if the female character shows them none. So, for these people, becoming a female is part of a strategy to use the natural or learned real-world constraints against hurting women to their advantage. Some of them have reported, however, that this strategy sometimes backfires because there are, in fact, natural bullies who are "turned on" by other people's "weakness" and who attack female characters more ferociously than they attack males because they see the females as weaker. For the most part, though, an adopted female gender works as a protective wrapping.

There are definite downsides to playing a female character, however. First is being sexually harassed by males who assume that they can bully a girl into revealing personal information about herself, and, second, is being treated like an incompetent by guys who will invite a female player into a group but then ignore her when the serious fighting starts, even though she is often a higher level than they are. More than one male player reported that he had just dropped his female character completely because this condescension and stalking had become too much to bear.

To try to tease out any differences between how male and female characters are treated in the game, I created two toons of my own one morning and sent them out as newbies to ask for information in a popular sci-fi MMORPG. My male character stood in the crowded town square and asked where the local portals to other parts of the game world were located. Through him I explained clearly that I was new to the game, but no one responded. I asked how the various professions worked. Again, no one responded. I asked if anyone knew where to buy better armor. No one offered a comment.

An hour later I brought out my female character, Sugary. Before she was even out of the training area, a male character named Dummy approached and offered to team up with her. When another character in our team crabbed at me for not healing him fast enough during a battle, Dummy rushed to defend me. And when Sugary entered the town square and asked her questions away from Dummy, two characters, one male and one female answered them immediately.

One striking discovery I made while cloaked in my new gender was that male characters would often step in to help me without even being asked when I was in the middle of a fight with a powerful monster. In fact, even when I was doing quite well on my own, they'd jump in to commit the *coup de grace*. After a while, their insistence on taking over, instead of just explaining how something was done, became rather annoying. I started looking for places to be alone when I went hunting or exploring. (I also sought solitude because I felt uncomfortable "leading on" male players who probably would have felt tricked or abused if they had found out I was actually a male player.)

Another discovery, however, was that the person answering my female character's questions was, more often than not, another female character. This took me completely by surprise, and I was never able to deduce why females were so willing to answer the questions of other females. Maybe it was due to a kind of "there aren't many of us here, so we have to stick together" ethos. Or perhaps the players behind the helpful female characters were actually male and assumed that they were helping a "real" female. Maybe female players are just more helpful in general. Or perhaps it had to do with the age of the helpful people as well as their gender.

This last possibility was born out by my long experiences as a male character. Never — not once — did a younger female character answer any question I ever asked — an experience that was quite striking. But older female players, taking on a more maternal role, helped me all the time. In fact, they became my most treasured information resources and guides.

Many older female players seem to be in the game for just this reason: to teach and to nurture. And, quite often, the most helpful players in any game are older female players, who often enter the game world specifically with the intent of helping other people.

Many of these players also admit, however, to a more subtle ulterior motive for playing. For some of them (women in their 40s and 50s) the game seems to present the opportunity to play the role of a coquettish young woman. This is never done cruelly to tantalize or trifle with the male players' affections. It's always a playful exercise, as if the female players are thinking, "If I knew when I was 20 years old what I know now, this is how I could act." Sometimes it even leads to carrying on long and passionate verbal romances with males in their 20s. For such players, it's almost as if the game is a live-in historical romance novel or a chance to relive a part of their lives with the upper hand this time.

By the end of my experiments I knew enough to bring out my female character whenever I had questions about the game. But the rest of the time I would play as a male. And I would recommend this strategy to anyone just starting out in a new MMORPG game.

On the other side of the fence, female players who had created male characters offered several different reasons for playing the opposite gender. Some trotted out their male avatar whenever they had to deal with male players who had shown female characters unwanted attention in the past. Some said they played as a kind of joke with groups of females because the male character in the group was always deferred to as the leader, even if he was a lower level than the females, and they wanted to see what it was like to be the leader all the time. And some said they wanted to spy on the all-male world to see what guys talked about among themselves. These players reported a definite difference in how they were treated as a male character, being "brought into the gang," "treated like an equal," "punched in the shoulder," and accepted in a way that they couldn't be as a female character. But they also said they had to be on constant alert not to mention things like baking or decorating their apartment or even phrases like "do something nice for him" or "cuddle" or other expressions that they thought would be seen as "girly." In fact, the act of trying to be "vulgar and violent" all day proved too much for some of them who abandoned their male characters to return to a life of reason and eloquence.

Not surprisingly, none of the players I spoke with played their opposite gender character as their main character. The largest part of their game lives was lived in the same gender they possessed in the real world. Most people said it just "felt right" or "was more natural" to play that way.

Maybe, in the future, when everyone lives one life in the virtual world and one in the real, this kind of research will come in handy. It suggests that people who are up to something, people who are trying to avoid detection, people interested in experimenting with their appearance, and people who see some advantage in falsifying themselves adopt new bodies. But people without ulterior designs often choose to recreate their real selves in the virtual world even when they may not be entirely happy with their real appearance.

And it also says something about the thought processes of MMORPG players. Some people are interested in recreating their real images in the false world in order to be more fully alive inside the game environment. This was a common comment from players. Many said it was easier for them to see themselves participating in game life if their character looked like them.

What's strangely interesting, however, is that the same people who chose look-alike characters didn't believe that appearance was one of the determining factors of success in real life. They always said that hard work, luck, or initiative led to success. Appearance was irrelevant. And maybe that's why they chose characters that looked like themselves — flaws and all. Because they saw appearance as irrelevant, they felt free to build characters that looked just like themselves.

Those, on the other hand, who saw appearance as a useful tool in getting what they wanted from other people used their character's appearance to benefit them in the game. And these same people *did* see appearance as important in real life. They believed that what you look like is crucial to getting what you want in life, so they falsified their appearance to get what they wanted. Not surprisingly, they were usually at a stage of life — teens to late 20s — when appearance is a perpetual concern in the attraction of a mate, so biological impulses may actually play a role in character creation as well. There's certainly a future Ph.D. dissertation here for someone.

That's Me When I Was Three Inches Tall

Most MMORPG players speak endearingly of their characters. And most will admit that their characters' actions align with their own personal beliefs and goals. They recognize their tendency to flame occasionally (use extreme speech or actions that they wouldn't use in real life). But they also admit that those flames are in keeping with what they believe about themselves and about the real world.

This seems to be because most players see their MMORPG characters as extensions or representatives of their real selves. And such a view is quite strikingly different from how players see their characters in other types of games.

In strategy games, for example, the player controls hundreds of little minions on the screen. None of these characters has a name, only professional designations: farmer, fisherman, knight, archer, miner. And none of them individually represents the player in the game. The player is their manager, their handler, their ringmaster. Only the collective action of the anonymous sprites represents the will of the player.

Players in traditional scrolling, overcome-the-obstacles games also have no bond of identification with their characters. Mario is not the player in electronic form. He's just a device, like a gun. He existed before the player arrived and he will still be there in his original form after the player leaves. He certainly doesn't belong to the player. The player didn't create him. The player doesn't nurture him. And anyone else who wants to make him jump on a turtle's back can bounce him into the air anytime they like.

An avatar in a MMORPG world is quite different, however. It *does* belong to the player. In fact, it can't exist until the player creates it. It's not just an anonymous muscle-bound cipher that gets pushed around on the screen. It's the player's ambassador, proxy, and cat's paw. It's the player shrunk down to three inches and instantiated into the computer.

The player forms the avatar out of nothing, breathes life into it, and imbues it with a personality. In a sense, the character *is* the player (only slightly cooler and far more focused on monsters and loot).

For some people, then, playing their character is like being translated into another language, a language that can be spoken only in the virtual world. For others, their avatar is a way of interacting with people in a different environment, an environment that can't be entered with the physical body. For still others, their characters are like the pseudopods of amoebae stretching from the living bodies of their players into the game realm. And, for almost everyone, their characters take on the same attitudes, convictions, and goals as the players behind them.

Avatars in MMORPG worlds become branch offices of the self. They speak with their players' voices and act with their players' intentions, so the personalities of the players spill right over into their characters. Abrasive people become irritating characters. Slippery people become shifty characters. False people become full-time liars. Good-natured, sympathetic players become helpful, easygoing, generous avatars. And this makes the game universe a microcosm of the real universe — subject to most of the same laws as real human life. In fact, the virtual world reflects both the good and the bad of the real world equally. For every character who insists that his good game self echoes the beneficence of his real self, someone else insists that game selves are really sinister versions of evil players' real selves.

One player, for example, was quite adamant in calling his game identity a purer, better form of his real self. In real life, he said, people might not like him because of what he looked like. Or they might avoid him because he had a speech impediment. Or they might not take him seriously because of his youth. So, they would never get the chance to know the real him. But, in the game, they did. And, if they liked his game character, they were liking the real person. Their opinion wasn't influenced by the shell of his real body. It was the real person they liked. The friends he had made in the game, he explained, were actually better friends than his friends in real life because they saw the real him.

Another character said just the opposite, however, after long and careful consideration. He explained that a real friend was someone who knows all about you and likes you anyway. He knows you're funny-looking and you smell bad and you're stupid and he still likes you because he can see through all of that. In the game, people only know what you tell them. And what people say about themselves and what they're really like are two different things. There's nothing to stop people from lying through their teeth every second of the day in the game world, so you can never know who a person really is in a MMORPG. All you can see is the fake self.

Hearing this, the other character insisted that this view was wildly wrong. In the real world people had to cover up or lie or exaggerate just to get through life. But in the game world no one had to do that. All pretense could be dropped. You could be your real self for the first time in your life in a MMORPG.

"If people who are basically good in real life," I asked, "are angelically good in the game, *and* people who are not so good in real life are truly evil in the game, then is the game amplifying players' real personalities? Maybe that's why people love their characters. Because they're more extreme versions of themselves. The character is the real person carried out to its logical conclusion."

"Yes," both players said immediately. One said people wanted to reveal their true good selves and the game gave them the chance to do it. The other said the game allowed liars and cheats and criminals to lie, cheat, and steal in the game to their hearts' content. So, yes, the game did amplify real personalities.

After long discussions with other players, another factor found to endear characters to their players revealed itself. It was the fact that characters grew and developed over time. This meant that some people regarded their avatars as their offspring, as if the characters had sprung from their own loins, or, like Athena, directly from the head of Zeus. These players invested huge amounts of time in assuring their character's well-being. They pondered their characters' future daily. They made decisions that they hoped would guide their characters along the proper path. They helped them live up to their potential. They put thought and energy into improving their characters' skills. They attended to their education. And they took their own roles as custodians of their characters' lives seriously, just as if the characters were their children. Part of the dynamic for many people, then, between a player and a character is certainly a form of displaced parental care.

And there may also be some element of friendship involved as well since many players develop a definite affection for their characters. More than one player said, "We've been through a lot together," about their avatars, as if they were talking about comrades in arms. This suggests that people are able to project their own egos into their virtual characters in the same way that they project their egos into sports teams, jumping for joy when "their own" team scores — even though they may not actually know anyone on the team.

In either case, the emotional connection that players have with their characters, almost a feeling of protective nurturing, may explain why some people stay in the game for so many years, growing and caring for their virtual personas, reluctant to abandon what they see as a child or a buddy or a part of themselves.

Many players also see their characters as a way of manifesting their ideas and ideals into an actual form. The character becomes a means of making notions about how life should work real in the synthetic realm. Most players are avid readers of science fiction or fantasy, for example, and they use the game to put themselves into the worlds they've read about. Many others are interested in creating entirely new lives for themselves, lives that are more poetic, adventurous, and lyrical than the real ones they're already living. And this ability to recreate themselves may also explain why some players become addicted to the virtual world. The game universe, after all, provides an environment where people can become their favorite fictional characters without taking on any physical risk, where they can live up to their own glorious view of themselves without physical restrictions.

Whether players see their characters as pure extensions of themselves, as their children, as their buddies, or as reifications of their own ideals, MMORPG characters acts as a powerful draw for many people and may actually hold them in the virtual world for years at a time.

—— *Chapter 4* ——

Attraction and Addiction

"Facilis descensus Averno."— Virgil, *The Aeneid*; translation: "The descent to Avernus is easy"; meaning: "It's easy to get into hell (but not as easy to get out again)"

"Everything is a dangerous drug except reality, which is unendurable."
— Cyril Connolly

The Purposes of a Virtual Life

Both players who are addicted to and those who are merely attracted to MMORPGs give similar answers when asked why they spend time in the MMORPG world instead of the real world.

First on the list is the fact that the worlds are "enveloping," "complex," and "nontrivial." There is so much to learn in any new world that becoming adept at all the different skills often takes months of trial and error. And mastering monster ecology, self-defense, quests, physical and financial survival, travel, pet taming, trade skills, map reading, salesmanship, and the social and cultural mores of the world is a completely absorbing experience.

Another very attractive aspect of MMORPG culture, as opposed to real life, is that MMORPG players are judged by their characters' actions, not by any advantages or disadvantages they may have in the real world. A person's game life cannot be accelerated or held back by any of the factors that accelerate or hold back a person's real life. And this makes substituting a virtual life for a real one an enticing possibility.

People with physical disabilities or those recuperating from serious illnesses, for example, can run, jump, and race in MMORPG worlds. Unemployed people worried sick about their real-world futures can find a sense of security and productive engagement in the virtual world. And people going through difficult emotional stretches in their lives can discover a sense of calm and triumph as they heal and recover from real life's assaults.

Many players find this side of MMORPG life thrilling. A MMORPG, after all, is a completely separate and egalitarian world where energy and resolve determine your fate and where appearance, age, connections, and socioeconomic advantage are all meaningless. In a MMORPG it doesn't matter how young and pretty you are, how svelte you are, what color your skin is, how much money you were born into, how well you did on your SATs, or who you know. The only thing standing between you and success is you.

So the game world offers a second chance for people who are ready for one. It offers the opportunity to start a new existence with no mistakes in it and no one to force them into acting in any particular way. And this, apparently, is an intensely attractive possibility for many players. It's the equivalent of getting on the boat to come to America or piling into the Conestoga wagon to head out west. In short, the game offers a chance to completely redefine and reinvent yourself.

Also, there's so much world to run around in that every day is filled with new discoveries. The enormous scope of the worlds draws in players who feel stuck in the shrinking, overcrowded, polluted real world. In many games, it's common, for example, for players to pause occasionally on a snow-capped mountain peak just to look out over the forests that stretch for miles in every direction down to the palm-fringed tropical beaches, parched deserts, and vast steppes. A typical MMORPG world spans at least 500 miles east to west and 500 miles north to south — covering more area than most European countries. So, there's enough raw geography available that players can do nothing but roam the game universe for hours at a time investigating the unique features of the landscape and exploring the mysterious hinterlands.

In fact, when the real-world economy suffers or when war makes the real world an unwelcoming place, MMORPGs are where many people now head instead of traveling on vacation. The virtual world is a place where wanderlust can be satisfied every evening. It's the place to spend whole days fording streams, standing under waterfalls, swimming in lakes, slogging through swamps, camping on endless wave-licked ocean strands, kicking up dust devils in the arid dunes, crossing mountains in the dead of winter, and exploring boundless continents that feel as if they've been set aside as nature reserves.

All of these factors suggest that people turn to the game world to fill in the holes in their real lives. They enter the game world because they're missing something in real life — a sense of adventure, social interaction, a sense of participation or purpose, the feeling of achievement, the chance to explore.

In fact, this is the obvious conclusion to draw when listening to people describe how much they prefer MMORPG life to real life. People seem to be running away from their real problems right into the virtual forest perhaps because they reach a stage in their real lives at which they're afraid of living, disappointed by life, or genuinely suffering. In a MMORPG, they can nestle themselves comfortably into a fake world to avoid having to deal with reality.

If this is the case, then MMORPGs fulfill the same kind of escapist role that movies, television, and music have always filled. But — unlike movies, TV, and music — MMORPGs don't just distract players. They actually offer the missing aspects of the players' real lives.

Teenage boys whose hormones impel them to break free of parental restrictions, for example, can roam the mystical lands and be independent for a change in a MMORPG world. People who are frustrated with their lack of effect on the real world can enter the game universe to exert some influence over it. People who lack mystery, romance, lyricism, or money in their real lives can find those things in the virtual world. And, disconnected and disconsolate people who may be painfully shy in real life can feel socially connected to a network of other players in a nonthreatening environment.

Everyone can feel a sense of accomplishment in a MMORPG. They can be distracted from severe reality. But they can also satisfy avarice, accomplish something, redefine their lives, and alter their foul or despairing moods. In fact, most of the forms of fulfillment or satisfaction that the real world fails to provide can be found in the MMORPG world. And that may be why people are attracted, and sometimes addicted, to MMORPGs. But it's not the whole answer.

When asked questions such as:

"Do you find your real life unfulfilling?"
"Do you have a tendency to avoid problems?"
"Do you look for ways of escaping from stressful situations?"

most players said they did *not* use the game as an anodyne for real-life pain at all. In fact, just the opposite. Many people had found their real lives busy, happy, and fulfilling before entering the game world. Their lives had overflowed with interests, hobbies, family, and ideas. They hadn't joined the game to escape. Instead, the false world had ambushed them. The game had inserted itself between them and real life and then immersion in the false world had provided the same rewards as real life without the risk of failure.

For many people, it appears, the virtual world is not just a way to fill in the blanks of real life but an easier substitute for certain aspects of real life.

The MMORPG life provides the same kinds of rewards that people seek out in the real world but it provides them in a way that involves less struggle and no threat of painful failure. People looking for beauty in their lives can wander over snowy mountaintops as the flakes fall and evening drops around them without having to worry about altitude sickness or hypothermia. People who are already creative in their real lives can create entirely new selves just by willing it to happen. Altruists and philanthropists can practice their beneficence in a place where someone nearby is always in need of assistance and can never hurt them in return for that assistance. And people who are shy but are still interested in interacting with their fellow human beings can do so all day long in a context that prevents anyone from getting physically hurt or even intimidated while dealing with other people.

The virtual world is a land where anyone can grow and prosper, where new ground can be broken in understanding yourself and your fellow human beings, and where the quest to figure out what you're capable of and what other people are capable of is accelerated because you meet people in difficult situations there every day.

So it's not as simple as saying that if you're missing something in your real life you can find it in the virtual world in such vast quantities that you may never want to leave. There are things to do in the game world besides fill in the deficits of real life. There are interesting ideas to explore, situations to experience, and perhaps even wisdom to gain. And those are such attractive possibilities that they entice millions of people into game worlds for years at a time, even people whose lives are going reasonably well.

Why Addiction?

Some people do become addicted to MMORPG life. And while the average amount of time that people spend playing in a MMORPG world is usually about 20 to 30 hours a week, there are, in fact, addicts — between 9% and 30% of the population, I found, depending on the game — who are in the MMORPG world all the time, day and night, weekday and weekend, for years. These are people who live their game lives and play their real lives. And they admit to immersing themselves in the false world anywhere from 50 hours a week to "constantly."

Part of the reason for this addictive use of MMORPGs may be that the worlds are set up in such a way as to appeal to the most essential wants and needs of the human psyche:

- the urge to get ahead in the world
- the urge to accomplish something
- the need to be part of a larger endeavor
- the urge to escape from harsh reality
- the desire to help others
- the urge to solve problems and make some money
- the wish to live a heroic life and grow by overcoming obstacles
- the need to interact with people without actually getting physically or emotionally hurt in the process and
- the urge to live in a world that makes sense.

If this is the case, then MMORPG addiction is really created by environmental variables that can be understood, controlled, and manipulated. Slot machines and MMORPG worlds are just operant conditioning mechanisms. They change the behavior of their players by rewarding certain actions. And particular forms of reinforcement are highly effective at addicting players. This view suggests that MMORPG worlds can be made so tantalizing that any ordinary person strolling by would be unable to resist their appeal.

But there may also be biological reasons for MMORPG addiction. It may be that certain people are genetically predisposed to life in the MMORPG world. They have brains that are hard-wired for repetitive, short-term pleasure seeking, even when it leads to eventual self-destruction.

According to this view, a variant of the DRD2 gene causes the creation of too few dopamine receptors in a brain structure known as the nucleus accumbens. People with this gene variant then seek out sources of dopamine to compensate, and they find that addictive behavior causes the brain to produce plenty of the neurotransmitter they crave.

When I interviewed players, I found that MMORPGs do, indeed, attract people with a history of addictive behavior. More than a dozen players in my initial interviews freely admitted (once we'd become friends) to a past involving the addictive use of alcohol, drugs, food, or gambling. And many of them said they had specifically chosen addiction to MMORPG life over other, more injurious forms of addiction.

The striking thing about these people was that they were among the pleasantest, most rational, most patient and helpful, least vulgar or cynical people in the MMORPG world. It was as if they'd come out of their past trials with a deeper understanding of themselves, a respect for the power certain actions could have over them, a greater sense of patience, and the inkling that other people might not necessarily be evil, just helpless, when caught in the grip of something they couldn't control.

But I also found that MMORPGs had attracted and addicted people who had no history of obsessive behavior. And yet all of these players demonstrated the signs of genuine addiction that are so common in MMORPG games that they help define the culture of the virtual world.

First, the more driven players admitted to neglecting their friends and families in order to spend more time with their virtual characters. Even so-called casual players were often embarrassed to admit this. Like gamblers immersing themselves in casinos, alcoholics in taverns, or pornography addicts on the Internet, some players consistently chose to play in the virtual world instead of spending time with their loved ones. They openly preferred the virtual world to the real world and they dodged real-life social engagement in order to spend more time in their MMORPG surroundings.

Second, both people who said they were "addicted to" the games and those who claimed that they played "quite a bit" admitted to arranging their daily schedules to accommodate their game lives. In the same way that drug addicts scheduled every minute around drug purchasing and using, many MMORPG players woke up early, went to bed late, called in sick, rushed home from work, and spent lost weekends in front of the computer.

Some players, even those who said they played as little as 30 hours a week, lied about the amount of time they spent engaged in their life-swallowing activity. They recognized at some fundamental level that the endeavor they were absorbed in was not conducive to a balanced and healthy life, so they felt as if they had to lie about the amount of time they were putting into their "hobby."

The self-admitted MMORPG addicts I spoke with said they often pretended to be on the computer for other purposes: reading e-mail, checking the news, writing reports for work, or surfing the net. If they were at home, they'd stay up late and wake up early to play. And they'd deflect criticism by hiding their actions, the way alcoholics hid their booze and drug addicts sequestered their secret supply.

Much of this happened because frequent players used their game lives as a mood alterant. It sounds odd to say that a game can be used in such a fashion, but consider the range of emotions available to someone ensconced in the virtual world. The wild and wooly combat atmosphere offers a powerful stimulant that completely envelops the mind and seizes control of the endocrine system. And the soothing social milieu offers a relaxing, stress-diminishing alternative to what may be a trying and aggravating real-world social environment. Add in the sense of greedy accumulation as the trinkets pile up, the sense of accomplishment as the previously intractable monsters fall to your growing powers, and the feeling of living inside a heroic universe where what you do really matters and where you cannot be severely punished for trying hard, and you've got the emotional mix that most human beings crave and often do not find in real life.

But certain dominant aspects of MMORPG life seemed to draw players into the virtual realm and hold them there. The satisfaction of instinctive desires, the chance to be enveloped in a compelling story, the sense of social engagement, the chance to be creative, the feeling of accomplishment, the opportunity to grow without falling back, and the feeling of having a thrilling job all keep people in the game for years at a time. Players who took their game lives seriously focused on these reasons for staying in the game world. And it's not possible to understand the attraction of MMORPGs without studying these specific reasons for abandoning real life in favor of MMORPG life.

The Lure of the Lore

One of the most enticing aspects of MMORPG life mentioned by a huge number of players is the lore — the story behind the game. But lore is not just the plotline laid out by the game developers. It's a combination of the game's premise, its monthly updates, and the extraordinary number of elaborations and contributions that the players themselves are able to add to the MMORPG world.

When I went looking for answers as to why people would spend years inside a game, many of the players said they relished the chance to be an instrument in the furtherance of the plot. The game allowed them to live out their own characters' escapades inside a kinetic book. And that's why they put their time into a MMORPG rather than into television viewing, radio listening, movie watching, or other forms of relaxation.

The premises of most games are actually quite rudimentary. Usually players portray characters who have settled a new planet and need to rid it of monsters before it can be civilized. But woven into this simple premise are extraordinarily long, convoluted, and multifaceted sagas — created by both the developers and the players — that enrich the game and raise it above the level of mindless creature-bashing.

Brothers wage war on each other. Despised archfiends gradually reveal themselves to be friends in disguise. Trusted allies turn traitor.

Power corrupts everyone it touches. Innocence dies and, with it, hope — until the players appear in the world to bend fate. They become part of the story that spins itself out over years of real time and involves thousands of named characters.

All of the subtexts, narrative twists, and filigreed story elements have an attractive power that many people — especially those who live on a steady diet of fantasy fiction — find irresistible. Add to that the fact that players help shape the fate of the world around them and that their individual stories become part of the game's lore, and each player feels like a tiny contributor to the plot.

This may explain why there are usually far more women players in MMORPG games than in ordinary video games. They run from about one out of 30 in PK worlds to one in four in more creative worlds. And the meaningful context of the game — along with the chance to establish connections with other people is what many female players say attracts them to the MMORPG universe.

In an ordinary video game, you race your Formula 1 car, blast every alien battleship that comes within half a parsec of your position, or lob incendiary bombs at the heads of bandage-trailing fleshless zombies rising out of their sandy graves. There's lots of adrenaline in these twitch games, but what plot there is can often be summarized in a single sentence. "You're a secret agent and the enemy wants to kill you." "You're a space pirate, so the empire wants to kill you." "You're a champion racer, so everyone else on the track wants to kill you." You don't really know anything about why the world works the way it does or how your own generic character fits into the world's events. You simply blast villains in a testosterone-driven slugfest.

The worlds of MMORPG, by contrast, are knee-deep in context. And the players create more context every day. They inscribe blank books with complicated stories and pass them around inside the game. They act as scribes and historians for their guilds. They get married in weddings that go down in history, complete with flaming invitations, dangerous bouquets, and scimitar-wielding groomsmen. Players at in-game events even read their poetry or sagas aloud. And all of this narrative creation attracts people who want to know *why* they're in the world and *why* they should embrace a certain role within the game. It attracts people looking for the chance to exist inside an imaginative setting.

One female player told me she found the chance "to live inside a myth, to be in a fantasy novel, to do the things I could only read about before" too attractive to pass up. An aficionado of fantasy literature, she played her character as a way of participating in an alternative life nurtured by the literature she immersed herself in.

Another female player, from Austria, had crafted her character from medieval Germanic legends. In the same way that Mad King Ludwig had surrounded himself with his Neuschwanstein Castle murals of a Nibelungenlied and Dietrichsage world filled with Valkyries and heroic warriors, she had surrounded herself in the game world with Siegfried-style warriors, Kriemhild-style beauties, adventure, glory, and escape from the mundane. "I'm living inside a medieval saga," she explained. "I'm one of the characters in the novel, and, at the same time, I'm one of the authors."

"Why don't you write the books you want your character to be in?" I asked these MMORPG-as-walk-in-literature players. "If you want to be in a book, why not write yourself into one?"

Many of them said that they did write lots of fan fiction. They wrote about their characters' lives and posted the stories on the Web. But mostly they wrote about why their characters acted the way they did in the game world — their history, motivation, and background. In the same way that authors scribble real-world autobiographies in order to make sense of their own lives, many people wrote about their characters to sort out their virtual lives. In the game world, protected by anonymity, they tried out actions, personalities, and behaviors that they couldn't try in real life, and then they wrote about them to understand their own true selves and to fit themselves into the context of the larger game world.

This kind of direct involvement in the lore makes a MMORPG a self-contained, wrap-around, involving, living experience that is even more engaging than reading a fantasy novel because your direct experience of the world reinforces what you read about it. Everything you do with your character fits in with the plot of the larger story and expands on the lore. And the lore itself enriches your actions in the world and embeds you in the game world's context.

This is what hooks many players on the game, even causing them to put aside their cherished books for a while as they sink into the mystical realms inside the computer.

Evolutionary Baggage

Another strongly attractive factor for MMORPG players is the undeniable pull of certain primal instincts. These include the urge to explore, the quest for survival, the need for independence, the wish to establish social ties, the sense of empowerment that comes from carving a path into the wilderness and making your own way in the world, the thrill of discovery, and the inner glow that results when you realize that you can take care of yourself and provide for others. MMORPGs offer a venue for the satisfaction of all of these basic human urges. And many people stay in the worlds for just this reason.

Ask MMORPG addicts what they love about their game and they'll often mention the very direct and primal sense of satisfaction. In the real world, by comparison, the connections between actions and results are often very indirect. You study in school in order to get a job where you type at a computer to make the money to buy a car to bring you to the supermarket where you purchase the food to feed your family. The connection between going to school and feeding your family is layers deep. In the game world, however, there's a direct link between bringing down animals and your own survival. And all of your Cro-Magnon hunting instincts are given play in this kind of world. Playing a MMORPG is not an intellectual exercise like playing chess or Scrabble. It's more like being the first person to walk on the shores of a new continent thousands of years ago. The continent is full of animals, and they're yours for the taking. You stand on the cliff edge gazing down at the herds and you know you're going to flourish. There's no feeling that is more addictive than this sense of discovery of the richness of the world around you and of your own competence and independence in that world.

Many of the players I spoke with mentioned that they owned reprints of the diaries of Christopher Columbus, the ship's logs of Captain Cook, the journals of Lewis and Clark, the travelogues of Marco Polo, or the histories of Magellan, Ibn Battuta, or Zhang He. They were fascinated with exploration. And MMORPG games were the closest they could come to discovering new continents on their own. In the virtual world they could be the first person to visit a new planet, the first to tread on a new island.

When I asked other players about this sense of discovery, one said he was a combination cave man, Indian scout, mountain man, and homesteader when he entered the MMORPG world. Another player said he'd rather be camping in the Rockies or living on a boat on a Pacific atoll lagoon, but that, at 50 years old and with kids to put through college, he was unlikely ever to do those things. The game world, he said, was the next best thing.

Many players mentioned these primal urges as their reason for playing. And none of the people I interviewed were hunters in real life. So, perhaps, the game was their way of exercising their ancient instincts to hunt and gather without hurting any actual living creatures.

The Human Maelstrom

Another significant factor in players' attraction to the virtual world is the form of controlled social interaction that MMORPGs offer.

Every time I asked a group of players why they played the game or why they felt as if they couldn't pull themselves out of the virtual world, one of the answers was always, "because of the friendships I've made here." In fact, for female players, it was far and away the most frequent response.

One player explained that being in the game was like being in the Stamp Club in high school. The jocks thought it was funny. They had no idea why anyone would want to collect used stamps. But the other members of the club understood the allure of philately while the jocks' passion, football, was a complete mystery to them. Why on earth anyone would want to put on a helmet and run into another guy for hours at a time and then relive the experience by talking about it later was beyond them.

Game life, this player explained, had the same shared-passion feel to it as Stamp Club or football. This is because the people in the game are not a random subset of humanity. They are preselected by the game, so a player can feel like a jock among jocks or a philatelist among his own people. Most players have enough of a shared worldview that they get along with each other inside the game better than they might get along with people in the real world who don't understand them. In a sense, the game acts as a computer dating service. It picks out exactly the people from around the world who would be most likely to understand each other's passions, and it allows them to get together and interact without any consequences for failure. Maybe it's only natural, then, that friendship would become such a large part of game life.

"What is it that people want from friendship?" one character asked me during a conversation about game interactions. They want to be included in a group, he said. They want respect. They want a sense of community. And all of those things are available in the game. People think the MMORPG world is isolating because players stare at a computer alone in the dark for months at a time. But actually it's the opposite of isolating. It's very inclusive. It's more inclusive than real life, in fact. And things like race and culture have little meaning in the game world because, in a sense, players communicate directly with the other players' brains and souls. So, for some people, it's a better place to make real friends than the real world, he asserted.

But I had heard so many joking "I need to get a real life" comments from other people that I had to ask some players the question, "Does it bother you that you have more friends here than in real life?"

Most people gave replies similar to those of one player who said he used to think there was something wrong with him because he had such a hard time making friends in RL. But after a year in the MMORPG realms, making friends everywhere, he had decided that there was nothing wrong with him. It was actually real life that was broken.

"But would you consider game friends to be real friends?" I had to ask. "You don't see them in real life. In fact, you may not even know their real names. Are they really friends?"

Friendship in the game *is* real friendship, everyone avowed. Just because you don't see the other person's real face doesn't mean the bond is somehow fake. It's real whether you meet the person in real life or not. Nothing about a real friendship depends on actually seeing the friend. Actions and language are the basis of friendship. Someone says a kind word to you. Someone helps you. Someone recognizes his own interests or even sees his own past problems in your situation and you become friends. You don't need a body for that. Having a friend in the game world is no different from having a pen pal in the real world. You may never see the person because he lives in another country, but the friendship is still real.

When my daughter took up the game, this was her opinion as well. In fact, one of her greatest delights was linking up with her in-game buddy and mentor, Granite, a female player who patrolled the deserts with her husband (real and virtual) and was happy to chat with a girl she apparently thought of as a kind of virtual niece. The association made both of them happy, and couldn't have existed in the real world where they were separated by thousands of miles of real space.

Everyone I interviewed, in fact, even the most misanthropic curmudgeons, said they'd had the experience of forming genuine friendships, often when another player appeared from nowhere to help them just when life in the game had become difficult and confusing. Some had been dead out in the badlands, armorless and unable to get anywhere near the monsters camped around their corpses, when a savior showed up to help. Some had been bankrupt when another player had offered money. Some had been utterly lost when a player had appeared from nowhere and provided directions.

Everyone could tell me about players who had gone out of their way to provide assistance and friendship. One player had skipped work for the day in order to help out a newbie suffering in the desert. Another had run into a spawn of villains to attract their attention just to help out a weaker character he had met on the road. The stronger character had then died as a result, lost the items on his own corpse, and had to call in his own even larger friend to help him, but he never complained. He even gave the younger player money at the end of the ordeal.

This sort of spontaneous kindness leads to close relationships in MMORPGs everywhere. A female player in one game world, for example, a mid–20s horticulturalist in real life, summed up the views on friendship that many players had expressed when she said that she hadn't gotten into the game to make friends. (Her boyfriend had been playing, so she'd gotten an account too.) But a year later she was still in the game world because of all the friends she had made. It was an unexpected benefit of game play. She liked talking to her gamemates, finding out about their lives, and going on adventures and quests with them. She said her boyfriend laughed at her and told her she treated the game like a chat room with moveable chess pieces in it. But she felt she had established a connection with the people in the MMORPG world. She shared things with them and they shared with her. She said that she didn't get enough of that in the real world — real conversation, real sharing. So she was happy to find it in the game world.

No Longer God's Toy

The number-one reason given by players for their attraction and addiction to MMORPG life, however, doesn't have to do with making friends. It has to do with accomplishment. The chance that games offer to get ahead and make some progress in life is a powerful draw. And the whole reward system of the games is designed to make players feel as if they're accomplishing something while they're playing.

The common misperception among nongamers is that MMORPGs attract two types of players: those who are hypercompetitive and those who feel frustrated and hobbled in their real lives. According to this view, players whose sense of competitiveness overwhelms every other aspect of their lives jump into MMORPGs in order to conquer everything in the game and beat everyone else, while people who find it too hard to accomplish much in real life get their sense of achievement from the game world.

There is some truth to this perception. When I asked one player, for example, a college student from Indiana, about the sense of accomplishment he felt in the game, he laughed. He said his girlfriend had told him that the reason he was addicted to the game was because he had flunked physics in real life. Playing the game was a kind of displacement activity, she had told him. He had been stymied in real life so he'd poured his energies into virtual life.

But when I asked if he felt that the year and a half he had put into the game so far had been a waste of time, his comments had nothing to do with displacement or real-world frustration. On the one hand, he said, he could have been watching soap operas with all his game time. Or he could have been getting into trouble at night. And he hadn't. So that was good. On the other hand, he could have been learning something useful or building something interesting with all his game time. If he had spent the time learning, he could have done better in school. If he had spent the time building, he could have produced something to admire, like a robot. Instead he was piling up fake money that would be worthless when the game ended. So it was a toss up. He hadn't hurt anybody, including himself. But he hadn't helped anybody either, including himself. He said he did *feel* as if he had accomplished something in the game, however, because he had passed through so many stages of development as a player.

This turned out to be a common view among players. Each achievement in a MMORPG— completing a mission, finding a rare object, helping a friend, defeating a monster never defeated before, rising a level — contributes to a player's sense of daily purpose and satisfaction with virtual life. Every player has a set of clear self-determined goals to work toward that seize the attention and absorb time and interest. And, strangely, the litany of purposes that most players go through turns out to be the same for a huge number of MMORPG players.

When they first start, for example, they are The Anonymous Noob. (I say "they" but my own character's path in every game also followed a similar progression.) At this level their mission is to learn the ropes without dying every five seconds, and they spend hours outside of the game world reading the manual and scanning Web sites to learn about the creatures and locations their character stumbles upon in the virtual landscape.

Then they transform into the Penurious Warrior, feeling stronger and more experienced but desperately poor and choosing challenges — quests, fights, sojourns, and monsters — based not on which ones will teach the most about game strategy or grant the highest XP, but which ones will yield the best loot.

Then they become the Power Leveler and camp a single spot for days, leaving only when they've risen from a low level to a mid-level.

For a few levels after that many players feel invincible. They become Miles Gloriosus, swaggering around and parading their extraordinary prowess, until they realize that most of the people around them are bringing in varieties of uberloot they've never even heard of.

Their purpose shifts again and they become the Explorer, roaming the countryside from end to end, probing all of the aspects of the game that had been mysterious to them.

When they realize that they can travel almost anywhere for the first time with a decent chance of surviving, they become the Adventurer, throwing themselves into harm's way just to see what they can withstand.

Then they often reach a Weary Traveler stage where the game suddenly becomes too easy. Every time they had experienced this sense of self-satisfaction and completion in the past something new had popped up to intrigue them and redefine their purpose for them. In fact, this is the way most people live inside MMORPG games: fascinated and enthralled with some intensely frustrating task for a while, then bored for a short time once they've conquered it, and then intrigued by a fresh goal.

But this time, they really feel as if they've exhausted the game, so they decide to call it quits. In what turns out to be an abandonment and return cycle, they often give away all their belongings and leave the game with no intention of ever returning, only to feel undeniable urges weeks later that prod them into reentering the world with a reinvigorated sense of purpose.

One player explained that he had quit after his main character, a mage, had reached level 50. Then he'd quit again when his new sword-swiper had made level 50. Then he'd come back and turned PK. But he'd piled up too many enemies. So he'd quit in disgust. Then he'd come back with the idea of becoming a billionaire. When he had five of everything he wanted, including mansions, the gum lost its flavor, and he spat it out. Each time he had completely quit the game, walked away, and closed the door. Half a dozen times. And each time he had felt as if he was being sucked back in again. His cravings became urgent. The game was like his cat waiting at the door, hungry and meowing. He couldn't just leave it out there. He had to bring it back into his life. The way ex-smokers dream about cigarettes, he had begun dreaming about the game world he'd abandoned. He'd had overwhelming cravings that he couldn't override with dispassionate thought, so he'd rejoined the game.

When players reenter the MMORPG world this way, they often realize that having seen and done almost everything in the game is actually an advantage. For someone needing information or help, they can act as a useful resource and a bottomless fount of information, weapons, money, and armor. And they often find a new purpose by entering the Sage Advisor stage.

This sense of evolving mission is certainly part of why many players become addicted to MMORPG games. Find anyone involved in a MMORPG and you'll hear the same responses. They keep playing the game because there's always something that *has to* get done. The game creates a sense of *I have to do this now.* I have to be somewhere. And it's not a someday "have to." It's right now. It's not, "I have to call my old friend from high school some day." It's, "I have to go to the bathroom. Now!"

And there are long domino chains of smaller goals that have to be met before reaching one big goal. To get the new title you *have to* croak all the monsters in the dungeon, for example. But you *have to* buff yourself first or they'll kill you. To do the buffs you need some mana. So you *have to* buy potions to boost your magical or mental power. But you *have to* croak some creatures with phat lewt to get the money to buy the potions to buff the armor to croak the creatures that live in the house that Jack built.

In real life you learn to walk, feed yourself, leave the nest, explore the world, dodge the bullies, make a living, recover from failure, find some friends, avoid danger, and exploit your opportunities. In game life you do exactly the same things. And, at each stage, you have different concerns. For players caught up in this system of evolving goals, then, MMORPGs become a kind of Hotel California. They can check out any time they like, but they can never leave.

The strange thing is that everyone in the game world knows that playing the game actually distracts a person from accomplishing anything in real life. When you enter the game, you put aside the sculpture you've been working on. You stop building the tree house. You drop your investigations into boosting the ambient-light-to-electrical-output conversion ratio of photovoltaic cells. You stop accomplishing anything real. But you *feel* as if you're accomplishing something useful every day because your character becomes stronger and you solve new problems from hour to hour. And that sense of growth and improvement is something you don't always feel in RL, so you stay in the more satisfying virtual world.

In one stroll through the hinterlands, for example, I met a group of players celebrating their completion of the Zombie Quest (collecting enough body parts and decomposing linen bandages to assemble a mummy costume). One member of the group had just abandoned a necessary diet, another had given up on trying to stop smoking, and a third had recently decided not to move up into a new position at work. And yet, here they were, jubilant at having found enough tibias and fibulas to attend the virtual Halloween party in costume. Even when the rest of their lives were not going well — or perhaps because of that fact — they had reason to commemorate an accomplishment.

"If you do things here, eventually you get ahead," one of these characters told me. He went on to explain that, in the real world, persistence and hard work don't always pay off because too many people get in the way. Sometimes they interfere intentionally out of resentment or competitiveness. Sometimes it's unintentional. But no one gets in the way in the virtual world, so it's a cleaner, purer world to work in.

Other players told me that their bosses decided what kind of work they would do in the real world — something they resented. Some said their "idiot teachers" decided whether they would get an A or not. Still others complained that driving instructors, parents, bank loan officers, judges, Ph.D. committees, credit bureaus, cops, or doctors all made decisions that affected their lives in the real world, decisions they themselves had no control over. And those decisions made by other people determined their fate.

But, they said, in the game world such interference doesn't exist because the game world is a pure meritocracy. You see your goals. You put in the time, thought, and energy to reach them. Eventually you improve. You rise in rank. You augment your skills. And you better yourself through your own diligence.

For independently minded people and those interested in accomplishment, this is part of the irresistible allure of the virtual realm. The game inserts itself between them and their real lives and allows them to get ahead without any of the obstacles present in real life. Purpose, mission, and accomplishment can be interlinked in the game world into a powerful attractive force that satisfies them in ways that the real world never can.

Let There Be Virtual Light

The chance for creativity is also part of the game's unique appeal for many players. And, when I asked around, I found large numbers of fellow players who all relished the unexpected and unusual forms that creativity could take in the virtual world. Clearly, the possibility for "doing art" was a big draw for these players.

In one world, I decided to test this notion by experimenting with an artistic medium that had never been used before in the real world: the decapitated heads of cat-faced monsters that had been filling up my backpacks. I laid them out in fractal formations in the town common just as night had begun to fall.

The sky was clear, but it was so dark that I decided to add flaming jack o'lanterns and reflective upright candy canes to the mix of objects that I distributed around the landscape. Laying out three intersecting rings of blazing pumpkins, with rows of barbershop-pole-swirled candy between the circles, I completed the field mandala before weaving a delicate filigree of severed heads in intricate patterns over an acre of mown lawn. It was part confectionary Stonehenge, part Celtic tripartite whirl, part Rococo embellishment, part Tibetan prayer painting, and part Daliesque clocks-melted-on-boulders reality distortion.

The people of the town were mesmerized. The reflected light of the jack o'lantern flames glinted off the polished candy. The white-furred heads, looking lost and lonesome without bodies, appeared animated in the jumping firelight.

One character spontaneously entered the nocturnal spectacle and assumed a meditative full-lotus position, hovering several feet off the ground in the center of the complex fractal pattern. Other players leapt up onto rooftops to gain a broader perspective on the landscape art. And I stood at the apex watching the whole scene gleam in the drippy yellow moonlight, the burning pumpkins casting their Plato's Cave shadows against the far buildings, the stalks of glossy candy rinsed by the light of the stars. I had to catch my breath for a moment. It was beautiful.

Someone came running into town and padded to a halt when he noticed the crowd and the startling beauty of the art around him.

"Woooo, what's this?" he asked.

"Performance art," I replied.

"Where's the performance?"

"It's me here. I'm standing here. That's the performance."

"Hmmm," he said. "Two words spring to mind."

"What words?" I asked.

"In. Teresting," he replied.

Then, for a moment, no one spoke. No one even moved. In a world where people usually spent every waking moment running, slashing, bludgeoning, pummeling, stabbing, bleeding, jumping, collapsing, crawling, screaming in terror, wailing in frustration, collecting, manufacturing, dispensing, yelling, selling, buying, and dying, everyone just paused and pondered the beauty of the odd flashing world around them.

For the first time, some of the players surely realized that they were inhabiting an artistic medium, a universe in which beauty could be created from fulminating rubble, in which the restorative power of fiery art could bring some balance back into lives otherwise focused on destruction and acquisition. Everyone paused, breathed, and almost sighed while gazing wistfully at the flickering firelight in the night around them.

Then, as quickly as it had captured the collective imagination, the scene disappeared. A low-level character, recognizing easy loot in a hardscrabble world, began picking up the luminous pumpkins. There was a free-for-all. It suddenly became dark. It looked as if someone had blown out the candles of an enormous birthday cake. And, in a few seconds, the lawn was clean again. But still no one spoke. As if they were reflecting on their brush with an alternative form of perception, as if they had realized that art was a way of looking at the world, as if they had been presented with a higher perspective that lifted them out of their daily lives and forced them to pause and reevaluate their mud-stuck view of reality, they just stood and pondered.

Someone put a flaming pumpkin on the ground in a kind of tribute to the original vast creation. For the longest time, lost in reverie, no one could speak. The experience had been lovely beyond words.

What I had discovered years ago when I was doing virtual reality research was that everyone went through the same cycle of behaviors while they were inhabiting a virtual environment—first exploring, then destroying, then creating. But, instead of working in oils or words or clay or tones, most players created in *behavior*. They created second, third, and fourth lives in which they experimented with their own responses to other people and difficult circumstances. And the same thing, it turns out, happens in MMORPGs where players re-create their own selves in a different context and environment. Their new lives become works of art.

One character, a Boston programmer in real life, told me that he saw the game as a big four-dimensional canvas to work on, and that it was the players who did all the important creating in the game, not the developers. He said he had created a character that hadn't existed before. He had created the character's looks, its actions, its purpose in the game, and its dialogue. And then he had enriched the lives of the other people in the game by interacting with them.

Another character complained that if he had written a book about his character's feats of derring-do, people would call that creative. If he had written a song about the character's actions, people would call that creative. If he had physically acted out the character's behavior in real life, people would call that creative. In fact, he could receive awards for any of those things in real life — Pulitzers, Grammies, and Oscars. Why, then, didn't people see that it was just as creative to make a character perform in the game world? A player could start with nothing and could come up with something complex and beautiful in an act of startling creativity.

How to classify this form of art is difficult, however. And even players who play chiefly to create, not to collect or kill or explore, have a hard time pinpointing exactly what it is they're creating. This may be because it's such an ephemeral form of art. When you're inside the virtual world, you're producing works that exist in attitude and action, but which go unrecorded. So they're more transient than any wind-blown Hopi sand painting because most of the artistry exists for only a few seconds at a time: a beautiful gesture here, a heroic act there, a noble achievement, a worthwhile deed, a clever maneuver, a selfless endeavor, an adventurous exploit. Each one of these lasts for only a moment and it may never even be seen by anyone at the time it is acted out.

The MMORPG life encompasses a wide variety of artistic perspectives, so there are lots of ways to interpret it. In one sense, it's a temporal brand of art, just as poetry is, because you spin out the work over time. Living in the virtual world is like writing an epic poem. Your character helps another player and that becomes one line: "He aided the unfortunate wayfarer who turned out to be Prince of the Far Lands." Then, when your character is attacked, that becomes the next line, "Forlorn and dismayed, he all but succumbed to the onslaught, finding barely enough strength to fend off his attackers." You don't actually write out the book, but your character acts it out when you're in the game.

In others ways, though, MMORPG life is clearly a form of stage acting. You create a role and perform it on the world stage. In still other ways it's a kinetic form similar to dance because you move through the world (hopefully with a little grace) and your movements are what people see and interpret. However, it's also creative in the areas of speech and relationship building in a way that dance and stage-acting aren't.

To top it off, the artistry can be different for each person playing a game. When my son played, his creative endeavors focused on altruism. He spent most of his time in the MMORPG universe helping people and giving away his possessions as if his character were a philanthropic character in a novel. My daughter, on the other hand, focused more on forming friendships and arraying herself in splendid garments. The world was a kind of walk-in theatrical production to her.

But they were both being creative in their responses to the new world around them because they were trying out behaviors that they would never have had the chance to try in the real world. Courage, initiative, exploration, compassion, fashion-sensibility, conversational skill, they were all there. And the structure of the game facilitated the process of experimenting with these behaviors because the interface introduces a layer of anonymity to social interaction. People can try on new behaviors that they wouldn't ordinarily attempt in the real world. They can create whole personalities for themselves and wear them for a while like articles of clothing.

Even players who don't think of themselves as artistic will often admit while strolling on a moonlit virtual beach listening to the splashing waves that the artistry of game life is a large part of why they play. It's not just that parts of most MMORPGs are strikingly beautiful. There are often Renaissance Tuscan hillsides to be seen, caliphs' seraglios, Remington cowboy scenes, Turneresque English impressionist panoramas of the foggy Thames, and Fauvist French Riviera tableaux everywhere. But game life also offers everyone the chance to create a new life from scratch — a beautiful and painless life this time — and that artistic possibility is intensely attractive to many players.

Spiritual Development and Religion

Strangely, there is actually a kind of spiritual development that takes place in the MMORPG world, a development that most people recognize but few verbalize. And this sense of spiritual growth may be part of the adhesive that binds people to the virtual world for long periods of time.

Not one person ever said to me that he played his MMORPG for purposes of spiritual enlightenment. No one admitted, "Oh, I play these games to grow emotionally, to develop my awareness of the universe around me, to open my eyes to beauty, to become a wiser person, and to learn about the human condition." But, for many players, the one thing that they do take away from the game on a daily basis is, actually, the sense that they are "making progress" on an emotional level. They're not just getting ahead in the virtual world, but actually maturing, growing, learning from their experiments with behavior, and reformulating their views of themselves and their fellow human beings as a result of their experiences in the virtual world.

Many of the more serious-minded players will hint at this expansion in their outlook, and some even see MMORPG playing as a growth experience. One player, for example, told me that he'd become a better person because the game let him become a better person. It let him develop a side of himself that he couldn't develop in real life. He saved people in the virtual world. He was heroic. He could give a lot of his time and energy to other people in the MMORPG. He could afford to be generous. He could teach people — people who wanted to learn. And he could use all of his best instincts, becoming a better person in the process.

This kind of personality growth is possible because MMORPGs are models for the lifelong maturation process of human beings. They're simulators of real life. And, just as in flight simulators, what someone learns in a MMORPG can be transferred into real life.

On the surface, this statement sounds, well, fatuous. But it only takes a few weeks inside any MMORPG universe to recognize the metaphors for real life that exist everywhere in gamespace.

First of all, a character's life in a typical MMORPG is very long — much longer than in an ordinary video game. A standard self-contained shoot-em-up is designed to provide about 60 hours of play. But a MMORPG often requires *more than a year of four-hour days* just to reach level 50. So your character changes over its lifetime and passes through stages of development as it ages, just as people do in the real world.

At the earliest stage of real life, for example, movement and communication are the goals. Just being able to walk and talk is an accomplishment. And it's the same in the MMORPG world. Learning to move around, converse, and pick up objects in the landscape are the concerns of beginning players.

Next, in real life, there is a long stage during which human beings educate themselves, venturing farther and farther from home until they are independent. Characters in the game world go through the same stage, developing skills and talents early on to aid them in later life.

Then they enter adulthood and, in both worlds, Maslow's Hierarchy of Needs begins to rule daily existence. People focus on physical survival and safety first. And only when those needs are met do social needs become a priority. After that, ego needs arise: self-respect, respect from others, confidence, and satisfaction. And then the higher order need for fulfillment emerges. People in both the real and virtual worlds are ruled by the same psychological forces.

During the course of their development, characters in both worlds pass through all the stages of adulthood that Carl Jung mapped out as well: athlete, warrior, statesman, and sage.

Athletes are fascinated with their bodies, their physical prowess, and their beauty. In real life most people pass through this stage in their 20s. In the game world, characters dwell in this stage from about levels 15 to 25.

One of my daughter's comments during this stage in her character's development was, "Look! I can run all day and not get tired!"

Next comes the warrior stage of adulthood when people strive to conquer the world around them. In real life, somewhere in their 30s, people take the focus off their bodies and plow their energy into career advancement, family starting, house buying, or the accumulation of money. In the game universe, when characters reach level 30 or so, they often focus either on getting rich or on "power leveling" schemes to make themselves invincible. They "get serious" about the game just as people in real life finally decide to "get serious" about their lives. Game players often decide that 30 levels of being broke and vulnerable is enough. From this point on, they're going to concentrate on getting ahead.

However, with eventual age comes perspective and a desire to return something to the world. So, in real life, the urge to conquer begins to fade in people in their 40s and 50s, and they begin to look for more advisory, mentoring roles as they enter the statesman stage. The same happens in the virtual world. Once a character has reached a level in its fifties, it has run every gauntlet in the MMORPG world and has amassed a huge amount of experiences that would "just go to waste" if not shared with newer characters. So assisting new players often becomes part of their game lives.

Lastly, people in real life enter the spirit stage where their concern is directed toward repairing the mistakes they can still repair, reconciling, forgiving, and contemplating the universe that exists beyond the self.

In the game world, characters at level 70 sometimes return to all of the people who had helped them in the game to thank them or repay perceived debts to them, while looking beyond the current game to consider the next game they'll be playing.

And, beyond the stages of single-lifetime human development, MMORPGs also act as allegories for spiritual development. Think of them as interactive *Pilgrim's Progress* stories or *Jataka Tales* for the 21st century.

This isn't as far-fetched as it sounds. If you look at life from a Buddhist, Hindu, or Taoist perspective, the lessons taught by the structure of MMORPGs correlate quite remarkably with the precepts of spiritual progress.

First, reincarnation is part of the game. You die over and over again, but you remain on the wheel of karma until you reach a high-enough level — a level at which you feel you've learned all there is to learn in the game — a level at which people finally leave the game world contented.

You also choose the circumstances of your birth. You create your character. You select your strengths and weaknesses. Then, as you play, you choose the challenges you will take on. They're not thrust upon you randomly by an uncaring universe or a malevolent god. You seek them out, consciously or unconsciously, in order to learn, develop, and grow.

Improving your character becomes a major purpose of existence. In the game world this means enhancing the talents and abilities of your virtual self. In the real world it means strengthening your own real character and working on your native talents.

And you can't commit suicide to escape your problems. You can certainly die on purpose. You can walk into a pack of befanged slavering arthropods who will rend you asunder and fling your body parts into the woods. But you'll just be reborn in another body and have to face exactly the same problems again until you solve them. You keep returning to the world to learn, grow, improve, and help other people. You die many times, but over the course of all your lifetimes you gradually become wiser and more compassionate toward the others in the same boat as you.

The goal of the game, in fact, is this process of self-improvement. It's not winning. No one actually wins in a MMORPG. Even the highest-level avatars can always improve. And events change so often in the game that there are always fresh challenges on the horizon, even at the highest levels.

Competition in this kind of environment is senseless. Some characters do make a game of outdoing each other in the acquisition of unique items, or the piling up of experience points, but since developing your own skills and helping others to develop theirs is what the game is about, comparisons with other players are really irrelevant. An improvement in someone else's fortunes doesn't diminish your own achievements in the least, so there's little reason to compare yourself with anyone else.

And one thing that is certainly helpful in the passage through game life is a friend. In fact, the more friends the better. Even if socializing and maintaining relationships is not your forte, there's certainly no benefit to mistreating people in the game. You may need them to help you fetch your corpse sometime. So, it's much better to remain on good terms with as many people as possible.

And, while you are learning, there is no limit to the number of lives you're allowed or to the types of approaches you can take to level up. You get as many lives as you need to learn your lessons. You're not playing against a clock. You're not playing against anyone else. So, slow learners and fast learners can all reach the same level eventually. And each individual player can reach the higher levels in his or her own way.

Just as there are many different yogas (hatha — bodywork, raja — meditation, bhakti — devotion, jnana — thought), there are many different paths to higher levels in the game — from the way of the laser beam to the way of the healing kit.

Both of these worlds, the game world and the spiritual world, also use the same model for learning — the opposite of the school model. In school, you learn the lessons first and then take the test. In the game, as in real life, you take the test first and then learn the lessons. You don't study Manglers first and then approach them. You stumble into the pack by accident and get clobbered. But, in doing so, you pick up useful knowledge that helps you progress in the future.

At the end of the game, when you finally decide you've reached a high-enough level and would like to do something else, you leave behind all the money and armor and goods and houses and weapons and trophies that you accumulated during the game. Trinkets that were fantastically important to you a few months before become meaningless. Ornaments that you stayed up all night to acquire, perhaps even cheated or stole to acquire, become valueless. Coins that you dreamed of every night for weeks suddenly become insignificant — just as they do at the end of real life. It's an inevitable part of death in the virtual world. And it's an integral part of spiritual life as well — the separation of the transitory and worldly from the eternal and meaningful.

Most players seem to take a moment when they finally leave a MMORPG world after thoroughly exhausting it, a moment during which they realize, *Sic transit gloria mundi* (So passes the glory of the world).

I asked one player what he was taking away from the experience of the game and he replied that he was carrying away lots of memories of people, interactions with other players, little kindnesses that other characters had showed him, and the friends he'd made while he was helping people fetch their corpses.

When asked if helping people was what he had spent most of his time doing, he said certainly not. He'd spent most of his time scrambling for money, killing monsters, and leveling up. But those things didn't really show up in his head now that he was leaving. He had thought getting more powerful was the main idea of the game and helping people was just something to do on the side. But it turned out, looking at it from the end of the line, it was the other way around. Helping people was what he remembered and all the stuff he'd had to do to get rich and get big he didn't remember at all. That part seemed like a waste of time, in fact.

Some players even experienced a sense of their own irrelevance in the game world as they left. Because they were leaving a game that was still going on, they realized that their own position would be quickly adopted by someone else. The water would close over them as if they had jumped from the world into a still pond. The waves would smooth over their exit point and it would be as if they had never lived, except for the good feelings left behind in the people they'd helped in the world.

Some players even passed through a regret stage when they left, just as people in real life sometimes do at the end of their lives when they realize how many hours they wasted at the office. "I could have written an entire novel by now," one player told me.

With all of these correlations between the stages of physical life, spiritual life, and game life, it appeared that what a lot of people were doing was using the game world as a practice space or a training ground for spiritual or emotional pursuits. Maybe they were learning life lessons and spiritual lessons in a virtual setting. If that was the case, then, MMORPG games might actually contribute to both the emotional and spiritual growth of the people who play them.

Think about that for a moment. People confront, work through, and resolve the same problems in the virtual world that they struggle with in the real world. They need to feed and clothe themselves. They need to decide whether they will act morally or immorally. And they need to learn as much as they can in order to survive and flourish. This means that the behaviors and responses they develop in the MMORPG world might actually inform their decisions in the real world.

Sometimes the responses of people to their virtual lives are negative: annoyance, pettiness, jealousy, greed, frustration, and competitiveness. And sometimes they're positive: joy, magnanimity, selflessness, forgiveness, gratitude, and kindness. And the same emotions are possible in game life as in real life. So the game world is not actually a fake universe after all. It's an alternative one that operates by most of the same rules as the real world and is filled with people governed by the same emotions and goals as in the real world.

After seeing all the stages of life reveal themselves in a condensed format in the game, players often gain a greater appreciation of those same stages in their real lives. And when they see that their virtual selves are not really separate from their real selves, when their virtual lives are really branch offices of their real lives, when their avatars are not objects to be manipulated but manifestations of their own thoughts and desires, some players even learn enough from their second lives inside the game world to improve their first lives in the real world.

Instead of being regarded as pointless distractions, then, MMORPG games might actually be recognized eventually as distilled and purified practice versions of real life. And, when players understand that the lessons learned in the game world are transported into the real world, the games might even be seen as the engines of emotional maturity and spiritual growth. Yet another reason to play all day!

In discussing this spiritual side of the game with other players, however, it became clear that some players saw the game not as a spiritual enterprise but as a form of religion. And the more players were presented with this interpretation, the more sensible it seemed.

All of the religions of the world have three things in common. They all provide a set of rules by which to structure one's life: the Eightfold Path of Buddhism, the Five Pillars of Islam, the Ten Commandments of Judaism. They all provide a set of rituals that bind together one group of people and exclude all others: doing puja, saying kaddish, going to mass, rolling out the prayer rug. And they all suggest a link between self and something far greater than self, a connection to something larger than one's own puny life.

These same three religious elements are offered by MMORPGs.

They provide a set of rules to guide player behavior. Some of these rules are codified in the form of the Players' Agreement (the "thou shalt nots"), and some are built into the mechanics of the game itself.

They also provide a wealth of rituals — everything from the "buffing" cycle (magical characters putting strengthening spells on themselves) to the daily cashing in of loot and refueling with food. And you learn these rituals quickly because you're scolded or ridiculed when you violate the taboos.

And the link between self and something beyond self is provided in a game by the lore. The backstory that underlies the entire game is replete with sinister reprobates and glorious saviors who struggle with each other on a plain far above the level of mere players. From their lofty perches these demigods sometimes preach a doctrine of transcendence — putting one's struggles in the virtual world into perspective. "We're all working for the common good," is a common lore sentiment. "Our fate is more or less laid out for us when we enter the world, but how we acquit ourselves while fulfilling it is up to us," is another one.

From a sociological standpoint, then, MMORPGs already have all the elements necessary to become religions in their own right. Perhaps it's only the growing wisdom of their inhabitants — wisdom gleaned in the virtual world — that prevents them from becoming such. Or maybe they already have become religions and we're just not calling them by their true names yet. There are certainly players who are far more devoted to the rules, rituals, and higher-order aspects of MMORPG games than they are to any organized religion. Maybe the games are already filling that role in their lives.

See No Evil

Another purpose the games fulfill is certainly stress relief. It sounds odd to say that frantically running from monsters who are trying to kill you is stress relieving, but confrontation with a different set of problems that act as a distraction from the real world is certainly one method of stress reduction. And part of the reason so many people spend so much time immersed in the virtual world is because it removes them from their real-world problems, serving as both an escape route and a recovery room.

When confronted with misguided teachers, benighted parents, destructive adolescent peer groups, manipulative media, bone-headed managers, self-serving politicians, job loss, rocky human relationships, war, illness, sadness, decrepitude, and the thousand natural shocks that flesh is heir to, who wouldn't rather slip into the painless, exciting, and beautiful virtual world? When the choice is between turning on the evening news (all bad) or turning on the game computer (all good), the decision is easy. When the options include pondering the state of the world or pondering the inanity of a character who strolls around for an hour announcing to everyone, "I'm looking for a cool wife, level 15+! A cool wife, not a nasty one! If she marries me I got a big surprise for the lucky gal!" the choice is also obvious.

In the real world, you get older, more tired, sicker, and more disenchanted every year until you eventually shrivel up and die. In the virtual world, you get richer, stronger, more adept, more knowledgeable, and more powerful every day until you eventually become invincible and omniscient.

In the real world, catastrophe can overtake your life in a single breath. One announcement from a doctor, one call from the police, one notice from the draft board, one moment of indecision behind the wheel, one pink slip, one SAT score, one death certificate, and your real life can spiral downward into oblivion. But in the virtual world, what's the worst that can happen? A monster conks you on the head and you lose your shoes. And what's the best that can happen? You stumble upon a beast that drops an item worth a million virtual dollars.

The MMORPG world seems like the obvious choice for anyone who wants to avoid sorrow and live a happy life.

MMORPGs provide the ultimate means of disassociating from the sad and punishing real world because they envelop players in a self-contained universe of growth, mastery, harmless danger, money-making opportunities, engaging history, thrills, and genuine companionship.

One player who had spent years in the hospital in real life, told me, "These games are the best method yet devised for mentally separating a person from pain without causing permanent repercussions." And, in fact, physicians at the University of Washington's Harborview Burn Center use virtual worlds to distract burn patients undergoing the painful removal of their bandages. Patients report pain relief of 40–50% while immersed in these worlds.

Anyone who doubts that MMORPGs are an ideal method of escape from reality only has to look at the alternatives. The catastrophic side-effects of taking drugs to escape extend far beyond the person taking the drug. Fantasy and romance novels require too much concentration to block the pain. It's common for people in distress, in fact, to spend entire nights reading the same line over and over again or reading whole pages without remembering them because it hurts too much to concentrate on the book. Movies are better. But because the story is laid out for you in a movie, there's no real sense of engagement to back up the sense of immersion. In the game world, you have to do something to gain pleasure and distraction from the experience, so it holds your attention more effectively.

MMORPGs are wrap-around worlds. You surround yourself with them. Their challenges are just difficult enough to keep your interest, but not so difficult that you become completely frustrated. And you derive joy and satisfaction from the game only if you actively participate, so you have to focus intently on the experience. You also control the story that spins out around you by deciding what your character will do at every given moment. That combination of direct action, plot complexity, engagement in the outcome, and gradual growth in understanding the game world's intricacies makes for an experience that completely removes you from real life's problems.

Some game players use this harmless addictive distraction to keep them away from other, more dangerous distractions. One player, a meteorologist in real life, freely admitted that he often spent eight hours a day in the game for just this reason. Protected by the anonymity of the game interface, he revealed that he had consciously chosen to become enveloped by the game world in lieu of addiction to more dangerous substances and activities. He regarded himself as having an addictive personality and had suffered physically as a result of other addictions. So, instead of trying to force himself to live without any form of obsession, he had gotten involved in the game world to satisfy his compulsive side and remove himself from harsh reality in a way that wouldn't lead to the hospital, the asylum, detox, prison, or the morgue.

MMORPGs may be this distracting because, in them, you can experiment with behavior as much as you like, learning about yourself and about other people, without being hurt in the process. More than one high school student told me, in fact, that they preferred the game to school because they had more friends in the game than at school and because they learned more about human nature in the game than in school.

The problem with this kind of appealing new life, however, is that it may dissuade players from actually dealing with their real-life problems. Spending six hours a night in the game world after eight hours in a rotten job may be understandable, but spending six hours a night in a night school course might actually lead to a better job. The same time spent in the game might be better spent exercising, reading, starting a new business, practicing strategies to overcome shyness, creating works of art, learning a second language, planning a trip around the world, or inventing things. There is, after all, productive distraction and non-productive distraction.

But the same years put into distraction in the game may actually benefit some players in a left-handed way if they prod people into realizing that time spent escaping from problems is not the same as time spent resolving them.

One player living in Hawaii, for example, said that if he had put all the time he'd spent in the game world into learning to speak French he could have been chatting up Tahitian girls over the net by now. He regretted the time he'd wasted in the game because he had nothing to show for it in the end.

But many other players said that the argument against MMORPGs as time-wasting distractions was silly. And they urged nongamers to look at what they actually did with their time in the real world. They watched many hours of TV — and not PBS. They watched golf, game shows, and sitcoms — not exactly mind-expanding fare. And 21 minutes of every hour on TV is now filled with commercials. So, one player said, it was obvious that six hours of strategizing in the forest was more valuable than a day spent watching *Green Acres* reruns and cell phone commercials. It wasn't as valuable as listening to Bill Moyers interview Joseph Campbell, he admitted. But he said that people couldn't be intellectuals all the time. And, given the choice between flipping through *Movie Star* magazines, watching tennis games on TV, viewing a *Mayberry RFD* marathon, or running through the virtual forests with their friends, he said he'd always choose game life.

And many people playing the game with their spouse, boyfriend, girlfriend, or children, said that even though the game world was an addictive distraction, it could, at least, be a shared distraction. Parents said they had more to talk about with their kids than just school when they played the game together. One mother of a college student said she played the game with her son while he was in his college dorm. It was their time to chat about his new life. Others said they played with their boyfriends or wives to bring them closer together.

In my own family, our conversations often revolved around a MMORPG we were playing together. It took no time at all, in fact, to provoke a friendly discussion in the house about game life. I'd commence, "Hey, I was in town yesterday and I saw this orb that looks like the earth with a moon revolving around it."

"Oh yeah," Jumbuck would say," That's the Auberean orb. It's part of a quest. Just go to Hub and ask people if they want to go on the quest. You..."

And off we'd go on half an hour's digression.

Then Bunyip would ask, "Dad, which is more powerful: a carrion shreth or a blood shreth?"

And off we'd go again.

Instead of me talking about work or them talking about school, we'd talk about a shared distraction, a common interest. And that fact lent some small value to the experience of playing the game for us. We might listen to different music, read different books, and watch different movies, but we could share our game experiences. And this use of MMORPGs as a shared diversion among people who are already close to each other in the real world is amazingly common among players.

Take This Job

Even more common is the use of the game as a substitute for an unsatisfying job.

In a lot of ways, game life is like the perfect job. Your objectives are clear in the game. You know exactly what it is you need to do. You don't have to read the boss's mind, scrutinize the subtext of managerial e-mail messages, or guess what the client wants. You're free from supervision. And you can be as creative as you like.

You also have all the tools required to do your job well. When you see that you need something new, you check the fan sites for a description. Then you go through the quest or negotiate the deal to get what you need.

There's no glass ceiling. There's no manager breathing down your neck or pounding the table screaming about deadlines. There's no time limit. You can explore and learn in your job. You can be creative. And you can be generous with your time and energy, stopping to help other people whenever you like.

The hours are infinitely flexible. In fact, you don't have to go to work at all if you don't want to. Or you can spend every minute at the job because you love it so much. And you can go to sleep concocting strategies to improve your game life and dwell, in your daydreams, on the struggles you encounter, working them out in your head first before trying them out in the pixel world.

You may have to cringe while contemplating another god-awful real-world day of crushing boredom opening mortgage remittance envelopes at your bank job. You may dread going in to see your halfwit manager scowling at you again for some screw-up she is secretly responsible for. You may curl up in revulsion at the thought of smiling through another one of your loony boss's screamfests. But you can still go home to your *real* job of saving the world at the end of the day.

In that job, you're well rewarded for what you do. There's a good mix of intense excitement and rejuvenating serenity. And, best of all, you're in control. You can seek out new life and new civilizations or somnambulate the afternoon away chatting with compatriots. And you know other players feel the same because, when you ask people about this, they always say they would love to "do the game" as their full-time job. They lol, of course. But they mean it.

"Gameful employment" provides the perfect substitute and antidote for the gainful employment that many people suffer through. Polls taken over the years show that, in most years, half of all workers dread going into work in the morning. And during recessions, that number skyrockets as people humiliate themselves to keep their jobs. How wonderful then to have a second occupation in the evening that provides so much of what a person needs in terms of purpose, goals, and rewards. No wonder MMORPG games are addictive. They give people exactly what they want but don't receive from their work lives.

Freud once proposed that love and work were the largest concerns of life and were the keys to happiness and health. And, in fact, a person's deep contentment with his work is the number-one determinant of longevity in the real world. If you love what you do, you tend to stay naturally healthy and outlive your agemates.

Maybe MMORPGs, then, give players the deep satisfaction that they don't get from their real jobs. Perhaps MMORPGs provide everyone with the chance to live the career of a superhero. Just as, during the day, Buffy is a typical high school girl, but at night she becomes the savior of mankind; and, during the day, Clark Kent is a mild-mannered reporter, but when danger calls, he becomes humanity's deliverance; the game job allows people who are middle-schoolers or middle-agers from 8 A.M. to 6 P.M. to become defenders of the universe after supper. And if it provides such a high level of job satisfaction, then maybe playing it even extends the physical lives of players.

A crucial factor for many players who regard the game as a kind of dream job seems to be that the rules of play are based on practical, not academic, knowledge. Many of the players I talked to mentioned this fact. They usually said that they loved learning new things, but hated school or work. And since the game world required no cramming or multiple choice tests, but did require learning to survive and flourish, it was the perfect job. In the game world you couldn't advance by means of the school-style memorize-and-disgorge method, sponging up facts and releasing them onto a test paper to rise in level. And you couldn't rise by the work method of buttering up the boss. All advancement was based on project-based trial-and-error learning that led to reasoned conjecture about the workings of the game world.

When I asked players what they wanted from their jobs in real life, they said they wanted to feel as if they were in control. They wanted to feel creative. They wanted to be taken seriously, to get better at what they did, and to move into new areas and not be stuck doing the same things every day. They wanted to make some money. They wanted to decide what to work on and when. And they said they could get all of these things in the game. Many people, in fact, said the game was the best job they could imagine.

So many of the players, in fact, felt this way that it was only natural that they would leave their "game job" reluctantly. The most touching moment I ever witnessed in the game world, in fact, was the final act of just such a player who had spent up to 100 hours a week for two straight years "working" in the game. It had become his second job and the place where he took his three weeks of real world annual vacation every year. Obviously, it had become a huge part of his real life's experience. It had not only engaged him, but helped define his life for years.

And he had become attached to his virtual character. So, when he finally decided to leave his second self behind, it was a wrenching experience.

Aching with separation anxiety, he went to the public market to bid fond adieu after a long and illustrious career in the game world.

"Im not sur wht Ill do wwith my time now," he lamented.

After an emotional pause he said wistfully, "Mybe il tak sum type-ing clases."

He stood in the market square not speaking to anyone in partic-ular, but soliloquizing openly into the virtual air about his exploits.

He recalled the time he had been swindled when he was brand new to the game. He had almost quit, but then another character had jumped in to replace all of his lost equipment gratis. In fact, a long string of selfless munificent players had graciously helped him when he was in trouble, giving him money, weapons, and armor, even running into the forest to help him with difficult corpse retrievals. He thanked all of those kind-hearted folks as he was leaving the game, even though he knew none of them were listening. It was as if he were making a prayer of gratitude, hoping the universe would pick up the smoke signals and waft them in the proper direction.

Then he launched into a final-parting scenario that must have been based on a half-remembered *Goodnight, Moon* bedtime ritual barely retrieved from the mists of his own childhood.

"Godbye Logout screen," he said as he clicked himself off for the last time.

He paused to get used to the feeling of not being in the game world any longer.

"Goobye Leave World buttin."

He lingered a moment, as if he were sighing to himself, as if he were mourning a loss, as if he were passing through the stages of grief while sitting at the keyboard.

"It ws so wunderfl here. My life ws so wondful. I'm goin to mss ths life."

Then finally, after a long silence, contemplating the "Are you sure you want to leave?" question that automatically appeared on the screen during the signoff, he took the plunge.

"Goodbye Yes button," he typed.

And then he was gone.

—— *Chapter 5* ——

Sampling the Games

"He felt that his whole life was some kind of dream and he sometimes
wondered whose it was and whether they were enjoying it."
— Douglas Adams, *The Hitchhiker's Guide to the Galaxy*

At the moment, there are more than 400 online role-playing games either fielded or in development. In fact, the joke is that in a few years there will be so many MMORPGs online that every player will have his or her own world to play in.

Each of these MMORPGs has a distinctive feel to it. Each features a unique combination of landscapes, challenges, player types, and emotional climates. And each attracts a certain kind of person. Some games rejoice in peaceful creativity and artistic freedom. Others celebrate bloodlust and human butchery. Some allow you to spend your time healing and teaching other players, while others let you ogle unclad prostitutes in store windows before shooting cops and drug addicts in the head during gang warfare. Some worlds allow you to live an avaricious life focused solely on business, competition, or thievery while others let you take the ascetic's path of devotion and poverty. The life you choose is up to you. And there's at least one world out there for everyone.

All of the games, however, share the common elements that define the MMORPG genre. In each one, for example, you can grow your own character through diligent effort, collect or make items, engage in commerce, go on quests, immerse yourself in lore, and form friendships with other players. But each game is different from the others in its focus, mechanics, and atmosphere. And even the smallest variation can radically alter the feel of a game, changing it from compelling to tedious. So it's worth opening the hood and looking inside any game before taking it out for a drive.

Generally, MMORPGs cost anywhere from $0–$60 to buy and another $70–$180 a year (in monthly fees) to play. To get the most out of them, many games also necessitate a multiyear commitment. So examining the differences between the games before jumping into any one world is a good idea. To help with this task, the main factors that distinguish the various games are listed below, followed by a look at MMORPG games of every style and approach.

The type of graphics that a game employs is the most fundamental distinguishing feature of a MMORPG. The games are divided graphically into isometric and non-isometric. In games that use an isometric viewpoint, you, as the viewer of the action, are positioned high over your character and the playing field. As a result, your character appears rather small (often less than an inch in size). And both your character and the landscape are likely to appear somewhat flat and cartoonish.

To many people, the isometric view (the same viewpoint used in real-time strategy games) looks like the perspective you'd experience from an airplane that follows the character around from a mile in the air. Games such as *Lineage* and *Ultima Online* use this viewpoint.

Non-isometric games, by contrast, strive for photorealism. They use a fully 3-D representation of the landscape and the characters, as well as an over-the-shoulder camera angle that follows behind and just above the character. Some of these games even allow you to shift to a bird's-eye view, a watch-the-action view (positioned in front of the character so you can see its face), or a first-person view (in which you see the world through the character's eyes). Games such as Toontown and City of Heroes use this kind of non-isometric viewpoint.

If you're considering the purchase of a game, pay no attention to the paintings on the front cover of the game package or the homepage of the Web site. They are usually artist's renderings and do not show what a game will actually look like when you play it. Instead, look at the screen shots for the game to determine if it uses an isometric view or not.

Balance is the second factor that distinguishes the games. Some games focus entirely on monster combat or player killing as the way to increase experience. In these types of games, there may not be much else to do except kill and talk about killing. Such worlds may turn into what MMORPG gamers call "a leveling treadmill" that forces you to battle all day for many months just to get up to a useful level.

Some people prefer this kind of game — a game that is consciously not balanced — because making virtual fish pies and sewing virtual tunics inside a game world seems deadly dull to them. But other players shun player killing altogether and quickly tire of perpetual monster combat, so they look for a more balanced approach to gameplay, seeking out MMORPGs that feature engineering, strategy, social interaction, or creativity as well as monster bludgeoning. Some players even look for games like *A Tale in the Desert* or *Second Life* that purposefully eschew monsters and killing in favor of peaceful and creative pursuits.

The social constraints of a game are also important. In some games you can flourish as an entirely independent character, never becoming beholden to other players for defense, healing, money, or anything else. And, though social interactions may be encouraged in these worlds (you'll receive more experience points when you're in a group), no one is required to buddy up with other people just to play the game. Both versions of *Asheron's Call* are good examples of worlds that allow for a more or less independent life while still encouraging sociability.

In other worlds, however, each race and profession has limitations that are severe enough to make a completely independent life difficult. In these kinds of games, you have to look for other people to work with in order to make any real progress in your game life. (If you're a healer, for example, you'll need to find people to heal.) *EverQuest* is the standard example of this kind of game.

And Player Killer games are also hard to play without forming allegiances with other characters. (A player on his own in a PK game is vulnerable to not only every monster in the landscape but also every other player in the game.)

Some people prefer the social entanglements of player killer and restricted race games. They welcome the chance to be bound to a group of other characters with different attributes. And the social system actually becomes a large part of the game's allure for them. But others find dependence on other players stultifying. They dislike having to mesh schedules with other players. And they look for games in which a masterless samurai can flourish without having to always seek out the help of other players.

The type of developer and number of players also have a large influence on gameplay. Most games at the moment are developed by large organizations. But there are games created by small groups of developers without big corporate sponsorship. And these often foster a close-knit community with lots of contact between the players and the developers (who sometimes spend their days inside the game world interacting with players).

The close developer/player relationship in these games allows them to grow organically according to the stated interests of the players. In one such game, *Endless Ages*, for example, the developers held a contest to allow players to design their own quests, and the winning quest was officially implemented in the game. In another, *A Tale in the Desert*, players regularly propose new laws that can then be voted into existence and folded into the game engine's rulebase. If you're looking for a game with a participatory or clubby atmosphere, these may be the kinds of games to investigate.

But the number of players in any particular game will also affect its look and feel. For people who think the hurly-burly and argy-bargy of crowded game servers make them feel more exciting and momentous, sparsely populated worlds often feel lonely and desolate by comparison. So these people seek out games with large player-bases like *Dark Age of Camelot* or *Anarchy Online*.

The number of players in a game also determines whether there will be a secondary auction market in the sale of game goods and characters. Small games just don't have auction sites with prices listed in real money. So a quick check on the number of players in any game may be useful if game play is going to be a profit-making endeavor.

Lastly, a look at any game's skill system and method of leveling will help in determining if a game fits with your interests. In fact, the leveling system is something that many experienced players of MMORPGs look at first. It has two components: the mechanism for acquiring new skills and the method for boosting the skills you already have.

In some games, you pick up "generic XP"—experience points that can be used to develop any skill. And you take on entirely new skills by rising one level, acquiring new "skill credits" and then choosing which new skills you'd like to spend those credits to acquire.

But some games, such as *Star Wars Galaxies*, don't use character levels at all and you gain new skills simply by employing similar skills (for example, when you reach a certain level of proficiency with a small blaster you're given the ability to use a larger one).

These types of games often use a "skill tree" to restrict which skills you can learn based on the skills you already have. A melee fighter in *Asheron's Call 2*, for example, cannot learn the "lunge" skill until he has learned the "flay" skill. In such games there may be thousands of skills, but very few of them will be available to you at any one time.

The system the game uses is important because the more leeway you have in choosing your skills, the more flexibility you have in developing your character. And how you build up a skill once you've acquired it is also something to study. In some games, such as *Earth & Beyond*, you gain XP in a particular skill (exploration, for example) just by using it. In other games, such as *Anarchy Online*, you gain XP with one skill that can be used to upgrade *any* skill. And in some games, such as the original *Asheron's Call*, your abilities in a skill increase as you use it *and* you gain XP that can go into upgrading any skill.

The way you spend your experience points in a game is something to look at if you'd like to have a powerful skill like healing but you don't want to have to spend all day doing it (which you would have to do if the only way to raise your ability was to use the skill).

Of course, many people choose a game because of its ethos, not because of its mechanics. They look for a lyrical New Age world, like *The Saga of Ryzom*, or one based on biotechnology, like *Anarchy Online*, or a world fashioned after their favorite book, movie, or pastime, like *Middle Earth Online*. Below are concise summaries of a wide range of MMORPGs to give some idea of the ethos of the various games. If you're just scanning for a new game to play, read the bullet-pointed abstracts at the top of each section first. But if you're interested in eventually building your own game or want to understand the diversity of game features available, reading the longer synopses will give you a pretty thorough reckoning of where the new technology and artistry of MMORPGs will be focused for the next several years.

City of Heroes:
(www.cityofheroes.com)

The distinguishing features of City of Heroes include:

- its emphasis on superpowers rather than weapons
- its focus on elaborate costume design
- its urban rather than space or medieval fantasy setting
- a lore system that allows players to participate in any of several different story arcs that wrap the player's character in the game saga
- and the game's comic book venue.

City of Heroes, from Cryptic Studios, is a MMORPG in which participants become comic book superheroes defending the denizens of Paragon City from thugs of all stripes: gangster warlords, menacing madmen, evil aliens, and cowled but uncowed criminals. In the same way that monsters are grouped together by species in other games, the dastardly heavies in this game are organized according to their affiliations with various underworld organizations specializing in the occult, bionic technology, or brute force.

The races that players are able to choose from are defined by the origin of their superpowers. There are mutants, for example, born with unusual abilities, altered humans who acquire their powers via life-changing scientific transformations, superior humans who have grown mighty through natural discipline and devotion, gadgeteers who acquire power through the technological tools they develop, mystic artifact wielders whose powers derive from ancient amulets and talismans, and those with magical powers who become adept at the practice of the secret arts.

The game takes place entirely inside the confines of the city — a massive place featuring a good deal of vertical real estate from the pinnacles of its skyscrapers to its sprawling underground sewer system. And the game's lore revolves around this city's role in an alternative history of Earth.

In this lore, the use of superpowered defenders by the British (the Dawn Patrol) and superpowered soldiers by the Germans (The Storm Korps) in World War II presaged future superhero organizations. An attack on Washington by the villain Nemesis after the war led to legal wranglings over the constitutionality of forcibly drafting superheroes into government service. And discrimination against minority superheroes, superhero dealings on both sides of the drug wars of the '80s, and the rise of the Russian superhero league from the ruins of the Soviet Union serve as a prelude to a modern era in which previously free-to-the-public superhero services are increasingly sold by corporations.

In this game you can act independently or band together with fellow caped crusaders to defend the city. Some of the powers that you have to choose from include the control of cold, fire, radiation, molecular density, raw energy, kinetic force, and the weather. Other powers provide you with strength, agility, invulnerability, speed, and flight. Throw in leaping, power punching, martial arts, clawing, and body armor, and you have a well-rounded set of traits for extraordinary individuals.

As one of these heroes, you are free to pick up missions from local hero organizations. These are slightly different from quests in most games because many of them feature both a long clock that starts once the mission is accepted and a short clock (often set to half an hour) that starts when the hero enters the specific location of the mission.

Failing to complete the mission before the alarm sounds results in a loss of fame points by the embarrassed superhero. But succeeding in the quest increases those points (which are independent of experience points), and allows the hero to take on higher level missions, adopt new costume accoutrements, and watch low-level villains run screaming into the night when they see your august presence stride into view.

The draw of the game is clearly the comic book setting, and anyone with a collection of *X-Men* comics in the basement is likely to be attracted to this game.

Earth & Beyond:
(www.earthandbeyond.com)

> *Earth & Beyond* is distinguished by
>
> - its emphasis on trading and mining, not just fighting, as the means of advancement
> - and its outer space venue.

In *Earth & Beyond* by Westwood Studios of Las Vegas, two hundred years of war has led to a precarious balance between the three races of Humanity. And when a stargate manufactured by an ancient unknown civilization is discovered, a corporation copies its design and the three races use it to spread out into the galaxy around them.

The Terrans, headquartered on Earth, establish trading corporations far and wide. The Progen, genetically engineered for battle, develop their pugnacity on Mars. And the Jenquai, philosophical wanderers, set off on their adventures from space stations off the moons of Jupiter.

When you begin the game, you choose both a race and a profession. Warriors focus on combat (ship-to-ship, not hand-to-hand). Explorers concentrate on mining. And traders engage in the buying and selling of goods. Progens are natural warriors, Terrans natural traders, and Jenquai natural explorers. But you can mix races and professions. And the most popular choice is, in fact, Jenquai warrior—a combination character that is not naturally belligerent, but can defend itself if necessary.

In most games, monster-killing is really the only way to develop skills or advance in level. Trade skills exist, but they're secondary and it's pretty much impossible to reach a high level employing only trade skills. However, this game's design allows characters to grow and prosper through mining/exploring and trading as well as through fighting. In fact, experience points are awarded along the three tracks separately: combat, exploration, and trade. This effectively raises what would be simple trade skills in other games to the level of major survival competencies.

Individual skills in these different areas are related to your class (in this case, the combination of your race and profession). So you specialize in certain abilities right from the outset of character creation. Skills are initially raised by use. But raising skills to high levels and receiving new skills generally requires the completion of missions assigned by NPCs. These missions may be chosen from among a list of "personalized" quests created by the mission generators located in space stations. Or they may be "crafted" missions that affect the game's lore and require the assistance of other characters.

Without a ship, however, your character cannot get into space. So, great emphasis is placed on the ship's design and function. Rather than draping your character's body in battle regalia, you spend your credits on designing and upgrading your ship — increasing its carrying capacity, missile power, and speed, and adjusting its energy pool and shield levels. You can only move your actual avatar around the landscape when it is inside "lounges" located on some planets and space stations, so all investigation of planets is done from within your ship, as is all fighting. You cannot get out onto a planet to walk around.

Travel through the vast distances of space is done from one nexus point to another. But close-up travel is through flight-simulator-style free roaming (as in navigating asteroid fields or in ship-to-ship combat). The celestial graphics — full of meteors, planetoids, nebulae, and asteroids — are quite beautiful. And the whole feel of the game is startlingly different from the forested landscapes of medieval games. The messages coming over the speakers in the space station, the planetarium music out in the void, the piloting heads-up displays, and lots of other little touches make the game very different from an elves-in-the-woods experience. However, the game can become repetitive because the experience of mining, fighting, or trading stays pretty much the same throughout your life in the game.

Those who are interested in a space venue, who are interested in playing a game that allows you to level up by a means other than fighting, and who are not fussy about long travel times between points in the *E&B* universe would be attracted to this game.

A Tale in the Desert:
(www.atitd.com)

A Tale in the Desert's most interesting features include:

- combat-free gaming
- a legal system created by the players themselves
- a landscape filled with the interesting creations of industrious and artistic players
- and gameplay focused on puzzle solving, exploration, engineering, creativity, and negotiation skills.

This is a game that emphasizes the gatherer side of the hunter-gatherer equation, and focuses on resource-finding, processing, and building, instead of monster killing. In fact, there are no monsters or player killers in this game. So it's for the person who prefers to solve, build, grow, create, and design, rather than slaughter. And even though the setting is ancient Egypt, it's really a kind of complex homesteading game.

Developed by eGenesis in Pittsburgh, the game focuses on a group of tradeskills called the Seven Disciplines Of Man. One discipline, Worship, requires you to coordinate the actions of other players in the performance of rituals. Another one, Thought, involves analysis and puzzle solving. The discipline of Conflict uses the dueling skills required in trading card games. Human Body requires you to explore and discover. Art focuses on the creation of impressive sculptures. Leadership tests your ability to convince other players to do things for you. And Architecture requires you to be good at money-making (needed to construct huge buildings).

When you've reached the highest (seventh) level in any particular discipline you can then embark on the next stage of gameplay, the accomplishment of a Great Work that uses your advanced skills in collaboration with other players to benefit the whole civilization.

The game's design encourages cooperation among players. Players interested in acquiring Leadership skills, for example, must find a newbie to tutor. And players who want to learn new acrobatic techniques (physical emotes) do so from other players. But most of a character's time can be spent in solo tasks without much problem.

New objects are created in the game through the use of tools in which players convert found or bartered resources (sand, wood, ore, clay) into more finished products (glass, charcoal, iron, pottery). And a typical player may juggle dozens of workshops at once and get involved in multistage processes. Pitching a tent, for example, requires planting flax seeds, rotting the stems in water, combing them out to separate the lint from the tow, spinning the lint into thread, and building a loom to weave the thread into linen. (Beyond the individual player, guilds may also own and operate workshops for their members, which can save time and energy.)

Once the raw materials are assembled, experimentation and practice are often required to pass the next challenge in the discipline you're working in. For example, finding the proper chemical formulas for fire-works and figuring out how to make complex and colorful explosions both require trial and error experimentation. Only when those things are done does the player participate in a test of abilities against other players. In the Art discipline, for example, a pyrotechnics contest takes place between players to see who can create the most spectacular fire-works. The winner is then boosted one level in Art.

This emphasis on player creativity in the game means that the land-scape of the world is decorated with player creations along every river bank, grassy valley, and mountaintop. Some of these are eyesores (min-ing equipment and kilns, for example), but many of the sculptures cre-ated by players are quite lovely — everything from 100-foot-tall Burning Man figures straddling bridges to dragons made of bound grain sheaves jutting from the peaks of mountains. This definitely enriches the game for both creators and observers in a way that is not found in other MMORPGs.

The rules by which the game is played are also far more democ-ratic than in other games. New laws, for example, are proposed by individual players themselves in the form of a petition. The player sug-gesting the law has to convince other people to sign the petition and, when enough inhabitants have signed, the game engine triggers a vote by all the players. If the law passes (by a simple majority), the devel-opers of the game change the code in the next patch to implement the new law.

Because the game is modeled on ancient Egyptian civilization, gardeners can grow grapes, cabbages, onions, leeks, carrots, and garlic. And scarab beetles can be bred to enhance the designs on their backs (making them more frightening or beautiful). They can also be used in a game called Witagog in which you give your beetles defensive and offensive powers and pit them against the beetles of an opponent.

Pets include camels, sheep, rabbits, and snakes. But their taming is handled differently in this game than in others. To "capture" a pair of camels, for example, you need to build a large outdoor pen for them and stock it with food. Every so often, the game engine does a survey of all pens in the world and the one with the most food in it suddenly finds itself filled with a pair of breedable camels.

Detractors say that this is only half of a game — the boring tradeskills half. And anyone looking for violent thrills should certainly look elsewhere. But *A Tale in the Desert* is likely to interest certain MMORPG players because many elements of its gameplay are quite intriguing. (And its innovative features will be widely "borrowed" by corporate game makers in the future for the same reason).

The ancient Egyptian desert milieu of the game feels genuine, and all the technologies (brick racks, kilns, skep-style apiaries, even the mini-games like Keket's Rake and Tug) fit in with the setting (although fireworks contests in ancient Egypt are a bit of a stretch). The players are also extremely affable, noticeably more helpful than in other games (though the world is huge and therefore sparsely populated). And the combination of passing tests of ability, keeping resource-processing factories going, and eventually performing "great works" all within the context of the storyline would certainly appeal to players who enjoy strategy games and prefer building things to destroying varmints.

Darkfall:
(www.darkfallonline.com)

Darkfall's most interesting features include:

- full-scale PvP territorial conquest (actual ownership of large areas of the game world)
- flexibility in choosing skills to develop
- and a rich system of hirelings (similar to strategy game minions) to do your fishing, mining, guarding, healing, and selling for you.

You can tell that *Darkfall* was created by a Norwegian game developer (Razorwax AS), just by looking at a map of its world. There has to be more coastline in this game than in any other MMORPG ever created. The world consists of one large main continent and three smaller ones, all serrated by fjords, bays, and beaches. And hundreds of smaller islands ring the continents waiting to be explored and conquered.

In some ways, *Darkfall* looks like a combination of traditional high fantasy MMORPG world and the board game Risk because the territory owned by your clan is marked with your escutcheon on the world map and because you can see which groups are making progress toward world domination and which areas are probably not safe for you to enter without an armed escort.

You are not limited in the amount of territory your clan can own in this game, so it is possible for one group to actually take over the entire game world. If Risk is a model, however, the other players will form temporary alliances to take down the big shot long before anyone can own the entire planet. But world ownership *is* a possibility — as is a global alliance of clans that results in a prosperous world completely at peace.

The available races include Alfar (slight, spry, and vaguely satanic), Dwarves (think Thor, the Norse thunder god, meets Hotei, the Chinese plump, lucky god of happiness), Humans (hmmm, they all look like Norwegians), Mahirim (tall, slinky, and wolf-headed), Mirdain (imagine Vulcans in Robin Hood attire), and Orks (a cross between hornless rhinos and the Hulk).

One consideration in choosing a race is that not all of these groups get along with each other. So racial wars are part of the game's overall structure. If you choose to become a Human, for example, you may be excluded from Ork towns by their NPC guards. If you become a Dwarf, you won't be able to sell your wares to Mahirim NPC vendors. And the Alfar hate everyone. So if you enter an Alfar town and you are not an Alfar, expect to be shot at.

There are no safe zones in this fully PK world. Anyone can kill you anywhere, even in your own clan's town, and the main focus of the game is, in fact, group warfare. But if you're not interested in killing people for territory you can make a living as a pirate and sail a galleon along the coast looking for merchant ships to plunder. You can also become a farmer, blacksmith, or even a trader who gets rich through arbitrage. (Simply craft a character from a race that is accepted by two races who hate each other. Then buy raw materials from one race and sell the finished goods to the other.)

Characters don't level up in this game. Only a character's skills level up (through experience). So what distinguishes a grizzled veteran player from a newbie is the number and sophistication of the skills acquired.

For most characters, there are no limitations on the types of skills you can choose to develop. You can, for example, pick up archery *and* sword swinging *and* magic all in the same character — something that is difficult to do in many other games where the paths of specialization are more restrictive.

You can also choose a specialized class (paladin, assassin, gladiator, enchanter, etc.) to gain certain unique abilities, but these come with concomitant drawbacks. (Druids can't wear armor, for example.) And your race can influence your skill caps as well. (Dwarves may be particularly good at smithing weapons, for example, but not as good as other races at spellcraft.)

But some of the skills you lack may be available on NPC hirelings that you can rent. These hirelings can heal you or dig for minerals, fish, hunt, patrol your town, or sell your wares. More useful than pets, and better than macros because they can reside in the world at the same time you are in it, hirelings come in different skill levels. The more adroit and adept hirelings cost more to keep on retainer. And hirelings that are killed and looted by enemies cost more to replace because of the greater risk to them. But they may be great time-savers and money-makers.

If player killing and group warfare are not what you're looking for, then this would be a game to avoid since it is certainly focused on group play and bloodshed. But players interested in working with large groups of other player-killers would likely be attracted to this game.

Toontown:

(play.toontown.com)

Toontown's unique features include:

- a completely kid-friendly environment
- the use of gags (physical humor) as weapons
- a strictly controlled menu-based system of communication that keeps all speech generic and non-objectionable until the player and/or the player's parents decide to open the system up to specific other players
- a series of mini-games within the larger game
- the ability to teleport directly to your friends by clicking on their names

- a log that records the types of villains you've defeated
- and the ability to use multiple skills/gags in a sequence (for example, to "Lure" a villain with money, and then "Trap" him with a banana peel).

The lore behind Toontown, from the Walt Disney Imagineering VR Studio, is quite terse. Scrooge McDuck wanders into the lab of Gyro Gearloose. There, he discovers a partially assembled robot. Connecting its wires, he sends it off to make money. But that one robot manufactures more of its kind and together the bot hoards try to turn happy-go-lucky Toontown into a gray and humorless mercantile city.

Your character — cobbled together from several of the classic cartoon "races" — dogs, ducks, rabbits, mice, horses, and cats — gambols through the streets in search of the Cogs, the robotic corporate villains who represent every form of downsizer, glandhander, and bottom feeder from annoying Telemarketer SellBots, to sleazy Bloodsucker LawBots, to smarmy Beancounter and Shortchange Cashbots, to power-mad manipulative Micromanager Bossbots.

All of these monsters — obviously modeled on real-life villains — have their own means of attack (shredding paper at you, sending fiery memos, wrapping you in red tape, flinging clip-on ties, wagging their fingers importantly, and hitting you with "the old razzle dazzle"). And they all keep up some form of obnoxious palaver while attacking you. The two-faced Doubletalker Lawbot, for example, shouts, "I know all the right people to bring you down!" The Telemarketer Sellbot sneers, "Is this a bad time? Good."

I can well imagine the game's designers, working in a part of Disney whose budget has been mercilessly slashed over the last few years, laughing uproariously as they molded these soulless corporatchiks. And I can also imagine parents who have to work in the corporate world happily jumping onto the game at night just to create a toon that can spit water on these vermin.

But the game is really designed for kids (who can read). So you don't decapitate blood-soaked satanic warlocks with silver halberds in this game. Instead, you "lighten up" the gray-suited greedy automatons with physical gags. This defeats them because Cogs have no sense of humor. When you squirt one with a flower and hurl a blueberry pie at him, he explodes like a clogged steam boiler because he can't take a joke (rather an ingenious bit of lore actually: eliminating villains without killing them, and using the villains' own failings against them).

When you start the game, you can choose your own name, or you can select a moniker from the generator that creates names such as Queen Roxy Whiskerbubble, Peppernose Spackletooth, Noisy Mac Marble, Good Ol' Dudley Frecklewig, Fat Jake Paddlemouth, and Spike Electrogadget.

And the game's design is just as much an amalgam as these names — which makes skill accumulation, money (jelly bean) acquisition, battling, and the layout of the terrain different from that of most MMORPGs.

The terrain is based on a modified linear system that feels like the traditional scrolling video game screen translated into a 3D form. Streets emanate outward from a central town square. Cogs of the lowest levels inhabit the near streets at the end of which you reach playgrounds. From the playgrounds you exit into tunnels and emerge onto other streets featuring higher level Cogs. The farther you walk, the higher the level of villains that appear before you.

When you initiate a battle by bouncing into a swaggering Cog striding pompously down the middle of the street, you drop out of real-time and a turn-based battle sequence is called up similar to the kind used in standalone RPGs (role-playing games). A menu of gags appears from which you select your "weapon." The game then shows you using the gag and shows the villain responding. Then, when you defeat the Cog, your character does a celebratory dance (hysterically funny the first time you see it, but a little tiresome after the 1000th time). Your accomplishments are then announced. Your skill statistics are upgraded. And your quest fulfillments are registered.

The skills you can acquire represent the different kinds of gags available: Throwing, Luring, Trapping, Making Sounds, Squirting, Dropping, and Tooning-Up (healing with tickling or joke-telling).

Most of these skills require ammunition. But you don't gain the money to buy ammo by looting your dead enemies. Instead you ride a trolley to a game-within-the-game system (reminiscent of Mario's detours for coin collection) that presents you with opportunities to swim through rings, shoot your character out of a cannon into a water tower, run through a Pac-Man-style maze, or play tag with another character. Your achievements in these mini-games gain for you the jelly beans you need to buy cupcakes, seltzer bottles, and squirting flowers to use on villains.

To help you keep track of your health and accomplishments, you have a Shticker Book that holds information on the kinds of Cogs you've defeated, the tasks you're currently working on, the skills you're in the act of acquiring, your gag armory, and the places you've visited. You also have a Laffmeter, in place of a health meter, that shows how healthy your sense of humor is. This is reduced when you're hit by Cogs and raised when other people amuse you with a Gag or when you play games in the playground.

When you "die" you shrink down to nothing and get sent back to the playground to recover your sense of humor. (Your only penalty is to lose your gag ammunition.) And teleporting to playgrounds or directly to your friends in the game is done cartoon-fashion by pulling a hole out of your pocket, stretching it and flinging it onto the ground to present a convenient manhole to jump into.

A great deal of thought has been put into preventing children from experiencing the unwanted attention of strangers through this game's communication system. And part of the solution is called Speed-Chat. It's a menu useful for kids with limited typing skills that allows players to communicate through a canned set of questions and responses. These include Yes, No, and Ok, as well as dozens of sentences categorized by purpose: Hello, Goodbye, Happy, Sad, Friendly, Sorry, Stinky, Toontasks, Battle, Gagshop, and Places (which includes, for example: Let's go take over a Cog building! Teleport to me. Where should we go? This way. Wait for me!)

There are parental controls that prevent the player from communicating with anyone except through this menu without parental permission. And another character can talk to you only by using this SpeedChat until you specifically put him on your Secret Friends list, a separate communication system you use to talk to your buddies in the game. To employ this system, you have to call up a randomly generated code word which you then send to your friend *outside of the game*. (This would have to be a real-life friend who is also playing the game.) Then the two of you can chat together freely using the keyboard while all others talk to you through the menu system. Clearly the game takes the safety of kids in a multiplayer world seriously. And it will be fascinating to watch how this kind of communication system evolves over time.

The turn-based combat and the restriction of the game world to streets and parks may feel a little constraining to experienced MMORPG players. But the color, whimsy, and clever elements of the game are likely to pique the interests of players tired of the standard MMORPG format. And for kids or cartoon-lovers, this may the place to start an exploration of the virtual world.

The Saga of Ryzom:
(www.ryzom.com)

The Saga of Ryzom is distinguished by

- its striking, otherworldly fantasy graphics
- its rich lore, which is different for each race and based on the principles of symbiosis, nature spirituality, and life forces
- an open source game engine that is available to others as part of the Free Software Movement
- an AI-infused world that creates a pronounced group-play game dynamic that shifts constantly, adapting the actions of hostile NPC tribes according to the responses of individual players, the guilds they belong to, and their civilizations
- and characters that grow old and have children.

The style in which the characters, plants, and animals in this world are rendered is reminiscent of the style of the French comic book artist Mobius and is quite lyrical and lovely. And the game's rich and complex lore complements the artistry of the images.

The lore focuses on Atys, a living planet on which there are no rocks or other inert matter. The entire planet (nicknamed Planet Tree) is composed of a living plant whose Primordial Roots are so vast as to form the mountains and valleys of the global landscape and to provide a home for the other plants and animals.

Each race in this world has its own way of looking at life and at the other races. And each has its own elaborate history, ultimate goals, and understanding of its place in a world where all food, clothing, weapons, equipment, ammunition, and art are made from living materials.

The races include Zorai, Mati, Tryker, and Fyro. The Mati are master botanists who selectively breed the creatures around them to serve various purposes, even raising plants to become forest homes and insects to become deadly projectiles. The Zorai, masters of the Original Energy, strive to cultivate balance through meditation. They find "management" of the planet's resources by the Mati abominable and sacrilegious. The Trykers, impatient, cheerful, thieving swashbucklers, live on the resources provided by the sea, but also feel entitled to steal from the other races. And the Fyros, believers in discipline and training, are masters in the manipulation of fire and the use of wood to fashion the weapons, equipment, and shelter needed by their warrior culture.

The fauna of the planet consists of predators, herbivores, scavengers, and domesticated animals. And the villainous NPCs (all drawn from the four races) have grouped themselves into Tribes: Barbarians, Outlaws, Pilgrims, Fanatics, Mercenaries, Amazons, Secret Societies, and those who align themselves with the various biospiritual forces at work in the planet.

All of the plants on this organic world have some form of consciousness, but not all are benevolent. Among them are predatory plants, plants that can communicate with homins (humanoids), psychically powerful plants that can control the thoughts of other living beings, and Fleeting Plants that are bred to be used as skill augmentation devices by the Mati race.

The game economy revolves around rare substances such as Kami-Bast, derived from the living planet and manufactured into everything from rope to ships to armor.

And the AI in Ryzom is not just embedded into the 120-odd species of animals, 70-plus species of plants, and 80 tribes of NPCs that populate the game. It also performs an overarching role as well in maintaining the balance of the world at large. This is seen in the quest generation system that creates different tasks for the guilds and changes how villains spawn based on how the races are doing in the game.

This is a largely group-oriented game, so balancing how the groups interact with each other and the larger world is part of the game engine.

The game was developed by London-based Nevrax, based on their NeL platform which is available for free to everyone under the GPL [General Public License], and provides the 3D graphics engine, networking, and AI used in fielding a MMORPG online game. Use of the Ryzom game itself, however, is subscription-based, as it is with almost all MMORPG games. So you're paying for the unique content rather than use of the engine.

This is a game you'd play for the elaborate nature-centered lore and the lyrical graphics, but teaming up with others would also have to be on your agenda because, after you rise from the elementary levels, group play becomes more and more important.

Asheron's Call 2:
(ac2.turbinegames.com)
(www.asheronscall.com)

The most interesting and novel aspects of *Asheron's Call 2* include:

- its streamlined gameplay
- a sense of balance that encourages group play but also allows loner players to go solo without penalty
- an economy that is entirely player-based
- a set of quests designed to reveal fragments of lore in the form of animations
- and a graduated PK system.

Asheron's Call 2, from Turbine Engineering, is designed to remove all the time-draining trivia from gameplay so that players can get on with what they really want to do in a MMORPG world.

The geography of *AC2*'s medieval fantasy world is modeled after the still-popular and highly regarded original version of *Asheron's Call*, also known affectionately by former players as "the game that will not die." (The original intent was to phase out *AC1* as *AC2* grew in popularity. But as *AC2* grew, *AC1* remained incredibly "sticky" and is still flourishing long after it was meant to disappear.)

AC2's world is divided roughly into three islands of increasing severity. One is a hilly green landscape, the ancestral home of the Humans, who are crafty and maneuverable. This is the island you start out on and play on until you've reached a high-enough level to visit other islands. The second island is a jungle/swamp/rainforest for intermediate level players, one that is traditionally the home of the Tumeroks, fast and rhythmic creatures. And the third is an icy, mountainous island for the high-level players, once the home island of the Lugians, large, strong, and ponderous creatures.

On all three islands, wide-open areas of wilderness have been set aside for those who want to exercise their exploration urges in the game. And this landscape, rendered with a second-generation graphics engine, is quite beautiful. Shapes are rounded and smooth, rather than pointed and angular. And, with advances in shadowing, heat-warping, water reflectivity, and special battle effects, the engine clearly represents a step forward in MMORPG graphics.

You have three races to choose from: Lugian, Tumerok, and Human. And the skills you can select from are influenced but not determined solely by the race of your character. Every player, for example, can choose a skill tree that is based on the three warrior paths available to all races: melee, missile, and magic. But if you decide that you've made a mistake in the selection of certain skills you can untrain those skills (with some time and effort) and then apply the retrieved skill credits and experience points to the opening of new skills. This means that you're never stuck with a gimpy level 45 character that you would certainly build differently if you could redo it from scratch. You can also view your entire skill tree to see exactly which skills you already have, which you have yet to acquire, and what those future skills will help you do.

You're likely to use every skill you acquire in dealing with creatures because monsters in this game use a slightly more dynamic form of AI than those in first-generation games. Instead of attacking you each time in the same way, individual creatures can select from a range of different strategies during an attack sequence. The monsters still hit with a force that is based on their level, so you can't be surprised by a level three monster that fires level 90 fire bolts. But you can't always anticipate how a monster will hit you or how it will respond when you hit it.

The economy of *AC2* is player-based because there are no NPC vendors to do the crafting and selling of weapons or other paraphernalia. If you derive a weapon from the treasure system (loot it from a creature or take it from a dungeon trove), you can simply convert it yourself into its coin value without running to a town to sell it. But, as a result, most unique, hand-made, or quest-derived items may have to be gained directly through your own crafting or through barter with other player characters. You save time in this game by not dealing with vendors, but then you use that time dealing with craftsman players or crafting items on your own.

The game does allow player-killing, but its PK system is an amalgam of several forms of PvP play that allows for various degrees of belligerence all tied to the notion of antagonistic kingdoms. When your character reaches a certain level, for example, you can join one of the three official kingdoms — organizations that are derived from the game's lore and are independent of the allegiance guilds formed by the players themselves.

In most geographic areas of the world, no PvP competition is allowed at all. So, players don't have to worry about being ganked in the woods by other players while they're looking for loot and experience. But, in some places, players in competing kingdoms can engage in competition without bloodshed (commandeering forges, workshop buildings, mines, or other facilities for the exclusive use of that kingdom). In still other regions, physical combat with players from other kingdoms is allowed. And in certain free-for-all zones, players of any kingdom can attack players of any other kingdom.

Kingdoms are part of the lore of the game, and that lore centers on the reemergence of three races from underground bunkers into a sunlit world ruined by the centuries of warfare known as the Devastation. The full storyline, however, is not dispensed to players when they enter the world. Instead, a system of lore quests, called the Vault Campaign, allows players to receive audio-visual snippets of lore narrated by an Orson Wells sound-alike whenever they defeat particular dungeon bosses. To understand the whole saga of the world you need to conquer all of the Vault Campaign guardians of history.

Ordinary XP, item, skill, and title quests also exist (you can level up just by completing quests and never hunting in the wild), but they are not handed out by lingering town-based NPCs. Instead, they are triggered upon the death of certain creatures or discovered on ancient artifacts in the quest area. To be able to create saddles that instantly materialize a mount beneath them, for example, you receive the quest from the boss monster in a dungeon vault. You then slaughter three different species of nasties out on the charred plains, receiving from each a potion or an infected saddle. Then you use a recipe for combining the ingredients to make the rideable mounts.

Everything the developers learned from *AC1* about making a game that is fast and not full of numbing minutia is put to use in this version of the game. But the streamlining of gameplay has some curious side effects. Towns are generally empty, for example, because there are no NPC merchants in them, and players are much more spread out over the landscape of Dereth than in other games because no one has to congregate in a town to sell loot or pick up quests. This means that the little thrill of finding something interesting in a merchant's pack or bumping into someone you know in town is gone. But it makes *AC2* an ideal game for lone wolves and explorers who don't mind doing their socializing out in the wilderness or at guild sites. And the characters are well balanced against each other so players can take on this world as either independent adventurers or team members — something that's difficult to do in some games.

Lost Continents:
(lostcontinents.vrl.com)

The most interesting features of *Lost Continents* include:

- its H. Rider Haggard/Jules Verne milieu
- its focus on family play
- its emphasis on offering a more individualized game experience by splitting off small parties of players inside "private zones"
- and its tying of lore directly to each individual player's experience within the game.

Both the monsters and the races in this game (a game that seems to be perpetually in development) are based on 1940s movie adventure serials and 1890s pulp fiction. Think of everything from *King Solomon's Mines* to Indiana Jones to Dead Eye Dick to Doyle's *Lost World* to Tarzan. The game world is divided into separate continents that correspond with those of Earth and are inhabited by creatures from adventure and explorer lore: mummy kings, gorilla guerillas, rogue elephants, and scorpion swarms.

The character types you have to choose from are Warrior, Scholar, and Explorer, and each has its particular specialties. Warriors are handy with guns. Scholars are spellcasters acquainted with ancient mystical traditions. And Explorers are jacks-of-all-trades particularly good at dealing with puzzles and traps.

Quests, called expeditions, are where you acquire unique items. And an interesting feature of this game is that once you complete a particular quest, you may never be able to solve it again, so characters carrying quest items in the game are far more likely to have gotten those items for themselves than to have bought them from another player. In fact, if you're twinked by a higher-level character [if you're given an uber-item far above your abilities to acquire on your own] you may find that the item doesn't work for you, or even backfires when you try to use it.

You gain experience points and level up by defeating monsters, but you can also grow by solving puzzles, getting around traps, and completing a series of experiences called an episode.

You have at your disposal both talents — which do not improve with use — such as Acrobatics, Ancient Languages, and Quantum Theory, and skills — which do improve over time — such as Animal Handling, Cryptography, and Gunsmithing. And there are tradeskills needed to assemble various components to create useful objects.

Zones are used differently in this game than in others. In most games, zones are used simply to balance the number of players in each area. But *Lost Continents* uses them to give players a more individualized experience of the game. Huge areas of the world are set up as public zones in which large numbers of player characters can interact with each other. But certain areas (think dungeons) are set aside as private zones in which you see only the resident creatures and the few other player characters who may be with you in your group.

Inside the private zones, the creatures can interact with you in a more personalized fashion based on your own unique experiences with them or with others of their kind. Creatures may even address you by name in a private zone or recall your past interference in their lives. And a more customized storyline can be presented to you, so you feel more like a lone explorer and rugged individualist and less like one anonymous soldier in an army of players all hacking into the same herd of monsters.

Private zones also eliminate crowded-world problems such as kill-stealing and camping because the private zones make it feel as if only you and your party of favorites are inhabiting a particular area. No one else is there to shoot your monsters or grab your loot. And, because the severity of play is adjusted inside a private zone based on your level and your past achievements, you're not even required to bring friends with you into each dungeon (although characters with abilities other than yours could certainly be handy).

The database manipulation that makes private zones possible means that creatures can keep track of you as an individual, can know whether they've ever dealt with you before, and can recognize you as a known harasser of their kin. This kind of system means that traps and puzzles (called "reactors" in the game) can be presented according to an individual player's experience. If you've already used a secret passage in the pyramid to kill the zombie queen, for example, you may find it booby-trapped with a death pit the next time you enter. This makes it possible for each player — each individual adventurer — to have a unique experience in the game world.

Lore, as a result, is handled differently in this game than it is in traditional MMORPGs. In keeping with the game's whole focus, lore derives much more from the exploits of the individual explorer/adventurer than from the background interactions of story characters created by the game's developers.

Some elements of the plot line are universal. Every player, for example, is brought in as an adventurer by the Society for Extraordinary Exploration to investigate the strange occurrences taking place across the continents as ancient forces roil the earth, and six power groups struggle for control of the world.

But, beyond that, each player compiles a personal history unlike that of any other player in the game. The private zones that each player enters evolve each time the player completes an episode in that zone. But they change for only that player and the characters he brings with him on his adventures.

He may enter a zone and face insect men the first time, for example, but confront ancient astronauts the second and robotic minions the third. Meanwhile, his friend in the game may see her personal lore record her scuffles with dinosaurs, tangles with Skull agents, and battles against zeppelins. Lore in this world is much closer to reportage centered on an individual adventurer's accomplishments than it is to the elaborate fantasy novel narratives of traditional medieval MMORPG games.

The game (which is full of great ideas but has suffered repeated schedule setbacks and may never see the light of day) from Jaleco Entertainment, is suitable for group play, but its emphasis is on individual accomplishment and activity in small groups, so it's ideal for players looking for the rare game where a character is more than just one more anonymous clan warrior or melee fighter. And its milieu is perfect for families playing together.

Priest:
(www.gamepriest.com)

Priest differs from other MMORPG games in:

- its unusual setting which mixes the genres of western and horror
- its unapologetically bloody and violent game play
- and its focus on first person shooter (FPS)-style player killing and PvP mass melees.

Distributed by JC Entertainment of Seoul, South Korea (the city that many gamers consider the world capital of MMORPG game play because such a huge percentage of the population is so devoted to the genre), this "hard-*gore*" action-horror game is derived from a Korean manga of the same name. It's set in the American Wild West where the lore focuses on the actions of an apostate priest named Ivan Isaacs who has sold his soul and spends his days battling a fallen archangel named Temozarela.

The game is an amalgam is every respect. It combines the sense of being overwhelmed by the dark forces of the occult with the each-man-makes-his-own-destiny sensibility of the western morality play. It combines rugged individualism with war-scale battlefield slaughter. It features the traditional role-playing game elements: 30 different playable characters, 12 towns, leveling up, gaining wealth, and using items.

But it also has a focus on blast-or-be-blasted player-killing drawn directly from FPS games.

Priest represents an attempt to meld the gradual-progress game elements that make MMORPGs popular with the constant-killing elements of FPS games. It's meant for players who want a dark horror-inspired cowboy world and who want to focus on battling each other in large-scale wars.

Dragon Empires:
(www.dragonempires.com)

> Dragon Empires' distinguishing features include:
>
> - a meteorologically sophisticated weather engine that allows evaporation, wind, and tropical rainstorms
> - an emphasis on the control of towns by clans
> - and a complex economic model that includes features such as taxation, arbitrage, resource balancing, and trade routes.

Dragon Empires, by UK developers Codemasters, allows you to band together with others to control entire cities which then have to be defended. This defense, as well as the maintenance and improvement of the town, is paid for through taxation of the town's inhabitants. And inside the town there are both traders who visit from outlying lands (bringing resources and removing finished goods) as well as player craftsmen who run small-scale factories to produce useful items.

When all is peaceful, the town prospers. But disgruntled citizens can rise against haughty landlords at any time. And external attack by jealous foreign clans is just as possible. On top of that, bandits can murder traders coming into the city. Monster spawns can shift position and increase. And traders can flood the marketplace with goods that are far cheaper than those produced inside the town. Even sieges that close off the city are possible.

Game play is based on a sense of balance between all of these competing factors. Too much taxation by player warlords and the other players rebel. Too little taxation and the town cannot invest in infrastructure, so its goods become too expensive on the world market and the inhabitants suffer. Too much focus on guarding the city means resources that could have helped the population flourish are squandered on defense. But too little defense means the town is exposed to rivals. And always there are outlaw players ready to attack citizens on the open road, and traders ready to make a war profit by sneaking expensive goods into a city under embargo. With some of the flavor of a strategy game, a definite player-killer ethic, and an emphasis on guns-or-butter decision-making, this is a game for those looking for more focus on real-life strategizing and less on monster-croaking.

Neocron:
(www.neocron.com)

> *Neocron's* most interesting features include:
>
> - an urban cyberpunk and post-apocalyptic wasteland setting
> - the ability to drive vehicles, ride in them as a passenger, and man the guns in them
> - and a rating of Mature (rather than the Everybody or Teen ratings of most MMORPGs).

The lore of *Neocron*, from Reakktor.com of Hamburg, Germany, is rooted in the catastrophic nuclear wars that leave 28th century Earth a barren, desolate, and desperate place. Only three domed megacities exist in a vast denuded terrain populated by mutants and evil clan minions.

The main city is divided into different districts. There's a wealthy section, the Via Rosso, where you're likely to be safe. There's a middle-class area, the Plaza District, where most people live and work. And there's a red light district, called Pepper Park, full of drug dealers, strip shows, and game arcades (featuring holographic battlefields where you can train in combat skills without dying). There's also a wasteland sprinkled with secret corporate labs, communication facilities, and factories — all of which can be seized by the clans (including your own) battling for control of the planet's scarce resources.

The Earth is populated by people of differing factions, one of which you choose for your character when you enter the game. The Brotherhood of Crahn consists of monks committed to developing their psi powers while converting heathens to their way of thinking. They have a tenuous alliance with members of the Twilight Guardian movement who resist despotism and have committed themselves to democracy and freedom. The Twilight Guardians are resisted by both the reigning elite in CityAdmin and by Tangent Technologies, the weapons manufacturer that benefits from the current autocratic government. Tangent is on watch against the Fallen Angels, engineers and technological sophisticates who may be responsible for recent hacker attacks against the corporations. But the Angels get along with The Anarchy Breed, a loosely bound group of criminals, misfits, and freedom fighters who tend toward self-destruction in Pepper Park and are often employed by the Black Dragon Clan, a mafia-style underworld organization with close ties to ProtoPharma, the drug manufacturer.

All of these factions have their own safe areas and homelands which become your first home in the game. To get around you can walk or employ tanks, bikes, and jeeps, all with wheels, treads, or hoverdrive. And you can use the weapons on them to kill creatures or other characters in the game.

Your own designation as a good or evil character is revealed by your "soullight" which can be either positive or negative, and changes over time. If you kill someone more positive than yourself, you become more "evil." And evil characters are automatic targets for the police.

Characters come into the world with a Law Enforcer chip implanted in their bodies which prevents other players from killing them (or them from killing others). But once you remove the chip, player-killing is activated.

Fighting is either hand to hand (baseball bats and stilettos), by projectile (nail guns and flame throwers), or by psi spells (toxins and shock). And you can withstand attacks through the use of various implants (bone reinforcement, synthetic heart), and steroid-like drugs designed to convey useful powers.

Creatures include the expected post-apocalyptic snakes, cockroaches, and mutant rats, as well as mechanical cyberdogs and mech-turtles. But the real focus of the game is on the struggles between the groups.

With a concentration on drugs, crime, sex, and violence, this is clearly not a game for kids. But you'd think that a game with no redeeming social value would attract teenage males and anyone else interested in a bleak urban landscape and amoral society. Unfortunately, the game has many problems, including tedious gameplay, nasty players, and lag severe enough for U.S. players that it discourages them from continuing.

Dark Age of Camelot:

(www.darkageofcamelot.com)

Dark Age of Camelot's most interesting features include:

- lore that closely follows traditional Northern European sagas and legends
- capture-the-flag-style relic-stealing from competing realms
- combat "styles" that melee characters have to learn in the same way mages learn spells
- and special separate servers for hardcore Player Killers and for Role-Players.

According to the lore of the original version of the game, three territories are at war with each other: Hibernia, Midguard, and Albion. Anglo-Saxon legend holds sway in Albion. Norse sagas influence the people in the Viking territory of Midguard. And Celtic fantasy imbues the green land of Hibernia.

All eight of the characters that a player can create on one server (there are many servers) must be tied to one of these realms. And the realm that the player chooses determines the styles of clothing, weapons, fighting techniques, and magic available to that character. It even determines whom the character can communicate with because you cannot chat with characters from other realms. (This is because all players in the competing realms are de facto enemies.)

There are 15 races and more than 30 classes (based on the melee/ranger/healer/mage model) but combat classes are handled differently in this game because fighters have to learn styles of fighting (about 40 styles to choose from) just as mages have to learn different spells. Certain styles are particularly effective or ineffective against certain types of monsters, and some styles can even be "chained" together into combinations that yield higher damage. This raises melee combat above the usual "chopping down a tree" tedium to something that's as interesting and complex as spellcasting.

Hostility between the realms is encouraged in a variety of ways. Each realm has a set of sacred relics, for example, and keeping them safely on home ground guarantees players tied to that realm a small attack, damage, and spellcasting bonus. When the relics are stolen by a competing clan, however, everyone in the realm suffers and war parties result. To further encourage interrealm fighting, the developers have installed a system of "realm points"—accumulated only while on incursions into enemy territory. High levels of these points allow the player to perform certain functions—like using a horse—that a character would not be able to do if he stayed only in his own realm.

Quests in each of the three realms are based on the local mythology and may generate as much as half of a player's experience points in the game. (The other half usually comes from croaking monsters.) But not everyone involved in the same quest has the same experience because the steps of the quests are randomly determined by the quest generator. To keep everything straight, players are given a Questing Journal that lists the steps taken and needed for the quests they have accepted.

The penalty for dying in the game is the loss of some experience points (and usually some "constitution points" tied to your health), rather than the loss of equipment. But you can regain half of the XP you've lost by returning to the scene of your demise and praying at your own gravestone. Players with healer characters (cleric, priest, druid) can also bring back half of your lost XP for you.

DAoC, from Mythic Entertainment, is very much a warring clans form of game. So players looking for something between the free-for-all of a standard PK world and the monster-destruction-only of a non–PK world would be attracted to this popular game.

Anarchy Online:
(www.anarchy-online.com)

Anarchy Online is distinguished by its:

- futuristic lore
- individually customizable quests
- large number of professions
- extensive pet and morph system

- the use of tiny spaceships that allow players to fly over the landscape
- and direct player influence over the plotline.

Anarchy Online, created by the Norwegian company Funcom, is based on future conflicts on the planet of Rubi-Ka between Omni-Tek, the evil corporation that runs the world, and the rebel groups known as the Clans, who counter the company's corruption and malfeasance with sabotage and violent defiance. As a character you can remain independent or ally yourself with the corporation or the freedom fighters.

You have four "breeds" (races) to choose from when designing your character: Solitus (humans), Opifex (spies and thieves), Nano (intelligent psychics), and Atrox (strong androgynes). There are also 14 professions that range from skilled mystics, spies, and healers to melee and range fighters. (Because this is a futuristic world, rather than a medieval fantasy, magic takes the form of power focused through crystals that stimulates the behavior of nanobots, rather than spells sent through wands and scepters.) Skills include all the standard MMORPG skills but also include Spying skills such as concealment, perception, trap disarmament, and breaking and entering.

AO takes the use of pets to a higher level than other MMORPGs. And many of the professions feature the use of some kind of pet. Bureaucrats, for example, can create and command fighting butler robots. Metaphysicians can cause their emotions to take physical form and can use physical manifestations of their anger (in the shape of floating minions that look like inflated spiked pufferfish) to do their bidding. Engineers can construct powerful battledroids. And Adventurers can even morph themselves into the forms of the resident animals — everything from groundhogesque Leets to two-headed wolves.

The penalty for dying in this world is a temporary lowering of your skills, the loss of your equipment (which can be reclaimed at the insurance booth), and the permanent loss of all points you've accumulated since your last "cell scan." It costs credits to use the cell scanner (which preserves your current XP state), but if you die soon after having used it, your loss of experience points will be nil.

Quests, called missions, are chosen by the player at a mission booth. And certain mission parameters can be adjusted by the player during the creation of the mission. For example:

- The reward for completing the mission can be weighted toward XP or cash.
- The mission itself can be weighted toward individual or group play.
- The form the mission takes can be nudged toward stealth or head-on confrontation with villains.
- The likelihood of locked doors and traps can be encouraged or discouraged.
- The feel of the mission can be pushed toward chaos (monster foes) or order (human NPC foes).
- The mission's type can be adjusted to good (fetch something) or bad (kill something).
- And the enemies' use of mystical force (called "nano" in the game) or physical force (think guns and melee punches) can also be set by the player.

The lore is extremely elaborate, stretches out tens of thousands of years into the future, and in some ways can actually be influenced by characters within the game who change the balance of power between the corporation and the rebels.

Gameplay is fast and interesting. And there's a large player base for this popular game. The training setup is excellent. And players attracted to a futuristic game with a complex lore, a very rich feature set (including hundreds of uses of nanotechnology), and customizable quests would certainly be interested in *AO*.

Project Entropia:
(www.project-entropia.com)

Project Entropia's unique features include:

- a game economy based on real money, and
- an expensive pay-as-you-go payment plan instead of a monthly fee.

Project Entropia combines the notion of a space epic with that of a medieval sword and sorcery fantasy by setting its play on the newly colonized distant planet of Calypso. According to the storyline, Calypso was discovered by probes launched into space by pioneering humans.

The humans eventually settled the planet. But a catastrophic war between robots and people ensued, leaving the land strewn with mutant humanoids and renegade robots, as well as dangerous native fauna. Now, years later, humans are settling again, and your character is part of this second generation of colonists trying to tame the planet.

The lore allows for a wild and pristine landscape outside the cities which, just as in medieval games, is populated by threatening creatures. In this case, they're pseudo-dinosaurs (called xenosaurs), flying giant insects, pleistocene-style mammals, invasive mutants, and hostile robots. However, the temporal setting is the future, so sophisticated laser weapons are the equalizers.

There are no separate races in the game. Every player is of the same race — human. And each player account is allowed only one character.

The usual quests and opportunities for social interaction exist here, but the game's most striking feature is its economy. On Calypso, you buy supplies and weapons and use them to upgrade your skills along the way, just as you do in other games. But in *Project Entropia* you do this with real money. The game's internal currency (the PED: Project Entropia Dollar) is convertible to U.S. dollars, French francs, German marks, Swedish krone, Japanese yen, or any other real currency. You purchase the PEDs you need to buy your equipment with real dollars, and the game company takes a transaction fee of about four percent for the currency conversion from dollars to PEDs.

This use of real money changes how game play is paid for and makes every decision in the game a monetary one. Even deciding whether or not to team up with your friends becomes a financial decision because loot is divided evenly between team members, even if some of them use no expensive ammo and never hit the creature. Some people find this emphasis on money hugely distracting.

The running gag, of course, is that, because of the use of real money, the game will require 60 developers and 6000 attorneys to sort out all of the lawsuits. And legal actions are easy to visualize when a server crashes in the middle of a transaction, when one player cheats another in a financial deal, when a distraught teenager loses big at the casino, or when hackers break into someone's character to liberate all of its PEDs. There has already been one widely publicized outside-user scam to defraud players out of their passwords as well as a game bug that prevented players from gaining experience even though they were spending fistfuls of money to shoot at and kill creatures (a bug that went unreimbursed by the company). But a larger fear may be the clever programmer who finds the exploit that allows him to manufacture goods or slaughter mutants without using up supplies.

Project Entropia's lore and structure — which focus on allowing players to make money by developing a virtual planet — conjure up lots of heroic and enticing images. The Company of Gentlemen Adventurers establishing tobacco plantations in the wilds of Virginia springs to mind. The East India Company merchants shipping spices from India. The Hudson's Bay Company voyageur network stretching across interior Canada. Even the invasive settlement of both the Americas and Australia seem like models for how the game may evolve. But if any of these enterprises can be used as guides, the earliest entrants into the game will gain the lion's share of the money.

In Australia, for example, these people, known as lordly "squatters," seized the best land from the native population before other Europeans arrived. They then became rich supplying the new country with the goods it needed to prosper. And such a scenario is easy to imagine in *Entropia*— a game that looks to some like a massive pyramid scheme in which the early entrants become rich and the later entrants support them — where the early adopters drive the Cadillacs and the late arrivals drive the cattle. Money also attracts the interest of criminals, lawyers, corporations, and politicians — the dark forces of real life — so it will be fascinating to see how these real-life evildoers become involved in the game's evolution.

But the collision of cultures inherent in a truly international game is even more interesting to behold. The game is developed by Swedes who live in a well-ordered, socially compassionate, peaceful, homogeneous, and wealthy society. The precepts of the game suggest that its developers may view the rest of the world as equally rational and benign. But when Americans, who live in a society where greedy self-interest is king, and in a country with the largest incarcerated population in the world (an astonishing one out of every 32 adults in the U.S. is either in prison or on parole), the culture clash is likely to be shocking to all parties. Whatever eventually happens in the game, however, it's bound to be more revealing of the real world than the virtual.

And, from a practical standpoint, the game, from the Swedish company MindArk, has a plethora of problems. Generally, more than half the players in newbie towns are beggars, for example, asking for free equipment and not finding it because even though the game is advertised as "free" to download and "free" to play, everything required by a player's character — armor, weapons, ammunition, mining equipment, manufacturing blueprints, everything — has to be bought with real money.

And anyone who imagines that he can enter the game, kill monsters with his fists, and become a real millionaire by selling the loot back to the company should think again because every aspect of the game is designed to drain money from the player, not give it to the player.

First of all, there is no bare-handed fighting. Monsters can be damaged only by a weapon. And, if you choose a pistol or rifle, one cell pack with 1000 shots of ammunition costs one U.S. dollar. The killing of a medium-level monster requires about 250 shots (25 cents in ammunition). But the loot from the monster averages about 10 cents. So, it's not uncommon to spend $5 a day playing this game.

If your plan is to beg a sword from another player, you'll have to remember that all weapons not only cost money (and are therefore almost never given away by players) but also wear out over time and have to be replaced. And monsters regenerate health so quickly that you can't croak them with just a few hits, so melee fighters need expensive armor, not just weapons, to succeed.

To top it off, the game is virtually unplayable from an ordinary 56K modem in the U.S. Modem players often lag to the point where they cannot move when they walk into any area with more than three people. And it's possible to be killed dozens of times when lag slows you down so much that monsters suddenly materialize in front of you. You may also have to became accustomed to a dozen or more server disconnects a day if you're playing in the U.S. All of this makes the game a trying and expensive experience.

Ultima Online:
(www.uo.com)

The interesting aspects of *Ultima Online* include:

- a form of title/skill quest system based on the acquisition of Virtues
- the inclusion of macroing inside the game's own interface
- the use of Karma and Fame systems to gauge the reputations of players and regulate the PK system
- an isometric point of view
- and a large number of incidental abilities from pet taming to ship navigation.

Ultima Online, the popular game from ORIGIN Systems, was the first official MMORPG and has been in continuous use for more than five years.

The game engine uses a system in which skills improve with use rather than through the application of general experience points. And the type of character you become really depends on the types of skills you choose to acquire.

There are 48 skill types to choose from — everything from expected skills like archery, magery, and swordsmanship to more arcane ones like glassblowing, lumberjacking, musicianship, cartography, and begging. Certain combinations of skills qualify characters to be labeled as certain professions. Necromancers, for example, focus on dark magic (curses and pain infliction). Paladins are healers. Warriors prefer roughhousing. Magicians eschew hand-to-hand combat, preferring spellcasting. And Blacksmiths concentrate on peaceful crafting.

You can use your skills for good or evil but your actions will mark you as either someone to seek out or someone to avoid. Committing illegal acts, for example, such as stealing loot from a dead player's body, will mark you as a criminal. And killing an innocent player will mark you as a murderer. Both of these actions will make you the target of bounty hunting players and get you banned from town shops.

Characters, both good and evil, are marked through the use of a reputation gauge that assigns levels of Karma to all players. Law-abiding citizens, high in Karma, are listed as blue. Criminals are gray. And murderers are red. (Guildmates are green, and enemy guild members are orange.)

The killing of lawful citizens results in a reduction of your Karma, eventually leading to red status for your own character. But the killing of gray characters, evildoers, has no effect on your Karma. And the destruction of red characters, murderers, will actually raise it. (You may then sever the head of the murderer and bring it to a shrine for a bounty.)

The other form of reputation that the game engine tracks is your Fame. Taking on creatures, NPCs, or players of higher Fame raises your own. And the combination of your Fame and Karma determine the title you'll be assigned — from Malicious, Dastardly, Despicable, and Nefarious on the low end to Respectable, Admirable, Illustrious, and Glorious at the high end.

Dying in the game results in a two-step process. Immediately after death you become a ghost who can move invisibly through the landscape to find either a healer or a shrine. And entering the shrine or contracting with the healer results in physical resurrection, but your resurrected body then has to return to the corpse to loot the items dropped on it. (No items that you have insured are dropped.)

The interesting permutation on title/skill quests inside *Ultima*—called the Virtues — also sometimes makes use of Fame. In order to acquire the Virtue of Sacrifice, for example, you can give up Fame points to "redeem" a monster. The monster is vaporized (apparently sent to heaven) and your Fame points are reset to zero. But you then receive a title related to the Virtue of Sacrifice as well the valuable skill of self-resurrection.

Within the same Virtue system, escorting an NPC bride or groom through the wilderness or freeing an NPC prisoner can gain you the Virtue of Compassion which allows you to convey a greater amount of health on other players that you may have resurrected. Killing a murderer gains you the Virtue of Justice and allows you to protect other players from harm. And eliminating certain difficult monsters conveys on you the Virtue of Valor which can be used to call up "champion spawns"— groups of creatures whose destruction can yield a scroll of power (which can set your skill statistics higher).

All of these attributes — Fame, Karma, Virtue — apply to the individual player, but *UO* can also be played as a group game.

The joining of a guild, for example, allows players to commit certain acts that would ordinarily result in a loss of Karma (such as murder or theft) without penalty. Both guildmates and members of enemy guilds can be mistreated with impunity. So characters who want to kill other players without being branded a murderer can do so within the game's guild or faction system.

An interesting feature of *UO*'s guild system is that members can declare fealty to anyone in the guild, not just the person who brought them into the organization. And the guild member with the greatest number of loyal friends becomes the GM [guild master] — a far more democratic system than the feudal pyramid used in most games.

Guilds can declare war or peace on other guilds to allow their members to engage in PK activity. Or they can join one of four large-scale factions that relate to the lore of Britannia.

The basics of this lore are that the forces of good, represented by Lord British, and the forces of darkness, represented by Blackthorn, have divided themselves into four factions: the True Britannians and Council of Mages on the good side, and the Shadow Lords and followers of Minax (a kind of Lucifer character) on the evil side. Joining a faction also allows the player to kill members of antithetical factions without penalty.

The game also has an extensive pet system that allows certain monsters and animals to become mounts to convey you overland, guardians to watch your gear or your body when you've died, and fighters who engage in combat on your behalf. There are also various forms of hirelings who can work for you, such as the Tillerman who steers the ship you can purchase. (The ship acts as a means of conveyance for your friends, as well as a storage area, and also a means of transport to far shores and islands. Navigation is done through either a set of commands or through course charting using a map.) There is also a system of customizable housing and crafting that allows players to create their own items for sale or use. And macros (lists of commands written by the player for the character to execute) are built into the game itself, so you can automate some of the tedium of repetitive actions like fighting or crafting. All of these features help the game to rise above the limitations of its graphical engine and camera angle.

People interested in a rich virtual world experience and not bothered by an isometric viewpoint would probably be attracted to *UO*. It has a sense of balance between group and individual play, built-in protections for younger players, all of the standard features one would expect from a MMORPG, and lots of innovative features as well, but you'd have to be comfortable with the isometric viewpoint.

EverQuest:
(everquest.station.sony.com)

EverQuest's most interesting features include:

- an emphasis on player grouping and cooperation
- and a sense of balanced play.

You have 15 races to choose from in *EverQuest*, a very popular game from Verant Interactive, including Ogres (huge and simple-minded), Trolls (grubby and evil), Iksar (reptilian and belligerent), Vah Shir (feline and folkloric), Halflings (good-natured and impish), Barbarians (rugged and burly), Erudites (graceful and intellectual), Dwarves (strong and resilient), Gnomes (subterranean and mechanically minded), Humans (adaptable and industrious), and various forms of elves: Dark (hateful and selfish), Half (agile and flexible in their thinking), Wood (clever and nature-centered), and High (smart and magical). The characters generally considered evil are Iksar, Dark Elf, Troll, and Ogre.

The race you choose determines the city you first inhabit in the game. And the orientation (good, neutral, evil) of your race may determine how other characters and NPCs will respond to you and which areas of the world will be welcoming or unfriendly.

There are also 15 classes to pick from, including the more magical professions of Wizard, Enchanter, Magician, Necromancer, Beastlord, and Shaman; the more physical professions of Warrior, Shadowknight, Ranger, Paladin, Rogue, and Monk (think martial arts, not quiet prayer); and the more artistic, spiritual or healing professions of Bard, Cleric, and Druid.

The combination of your race and class will determine your starting attributes (e.g., strength, wisdom, charisma).

There are 40 skills to choose from, including:

- the magical skills such as Alchemy, Divination, and Meditate;
- the fighting skills such as Dodge, Flying Kick, and Melee Weapons;

- and the miscellaneous skills of Singing, Foraging, and Backstabbing.

There are also plenty of trade skills, including jewelry-making, pottery-throwing, brewing, fletching, baking, blacksmithing, tinkering, tailoring, poison-making, and fishing.

Your last choice in character development involves the Deity your character worships in the game. Some are good and some are evil. And this Deity, as well as your Race and Class, can affect your experience of the game because certain items can be worn or used only by players with a certain Deity, Race, or Class.

The limitations on your abilities placed on you by your character traits mean that you may be unable to take down monsters on your own in certain situations. So, the game nudges you in the direction of teaming up with other players who have strengths that compensate for your weaknesses.

These groups can be formalized through the creation of guilds and anyone can start a guild. But there must be 10 other players willing to petition the game engine for membership. If the petition is accepted, the guild members, now bound in the same group, find it easier to communicate and work with those in the group.

There is no penalty for dying up to Level 10. But then experience points are subtracted after death (the higher the level the more points lost), and a character can drop a level as a result. You'll also drop equipment upon your demise.

And you can become PK by turning in a book called the Tome of Discord. But PKs are not common on the servers that are not specifically set up for PKs. And, as a result, game play is much less fear-and-hostility-based than in games that encourage pickpocketing, stealing, and murder.

As most MMORPGs do, *EQ* has a separate server set up for free-for-all PK players. It also has servers for team-oriented PK and for role-players.

The economy is both NPC-based and player-based. You're likely to spend time with merchants at early levels, but trade rare goods with fellow players at higher levels.

There are five large island continents in the world of Norrath, each with its own unique ecology and historical ties to certain races. And monsters spawn in certain places on those islands with enough regularity that camping (sitting and waiting for creatures to rematerialize) is the most common subject of complaints in the game.

EverQuest is a very balanced game in terms of its features — which may explain its popularity and addictive power. It does not emphasize clan wars or PK bloodlust (outside the PK servers). It has spawned off a large real-world auction market for in-game items. And cooperation between players is encouraged by the structure of the Race/Class/Deity system. It's not really a game for loners who prefer to solo, but players interested in the game's sense of balance and not bothered by the camping, crowding, and time required to change zones would probably be attracted to *EverQuest*.

Lineage:
(www.lineage-us.com)

Lineage's interesting features include:

- an underwater realm for adventuring and battling
- an isometric viewpoint
- a controversial royal race
- and a way of bookmarking and teleporting to specific places your character has visited.

With millions of active subscribers, *Lineage* is currently the most popular MMORPG in the world, although it is not well known outside of Asia. Created by NCSoft in South Korea (where the game is something of a national phenomenon) *Lineage*'s world of Aden is a medieval realm of monsters, dragons, forests, castles, and kingdom-wide warfare.

You have four classes to choose from when creating your character — one of which has been controversial outside of the game's main territories of Korea, China, and Japan, and does not seem to exist in any games created in the West.

Players can become:

- Wizards (physically weak but magically powerfully)
- Knights (physically powerful but magically inept)

- Elves (well-rounded ranger characters with some magic, some weapon skills, and some unique abilities), and
- Princes/Princesses (not very skilled at anything, but the only characters allowed to rule a territory, command others, lead sieges, wage wars, or assemble pledge members (form a guild).

It's this last category that has been the subject of discussion among Western gamers. Some view this race of ruling elites as contrary to the whole idea of self-determination in a game. And some gamers have complained that the existence of a lordly class limits their game play — forcing them to either accept grunt status for their entire game lives as wizards, knights, or elves, or to accept a character type (the Royal) that is severely restricted in its abilities from the start.

Besides race, there is one more trait that characters have to consider as they grow inside the game: alignment. Characters who kill only evil creatures push their alignment toward good and "lawful." Those who kill good creatures (including harmless NPCs) push themselves toward evil and "chaotic." These chaotics then become the target of NPC guards, and they can also be killed by lawful players who will be given bonus points for helping rid the world of evil.

To get away from the people chasing you, you may have to teleport away. In most games you do this by entering a portal entrance in one place that brings you to another part of the landscape. In some games, you can even use a gem or a spell to bring you somewhere. But in this game you also have one more option for travel. You can bookmark a spot as you travel through it and teleport back to that waypoint later on.

Dying in this game can result in the loss of both experience points and items (though you won't drop items if you are fully lawful). The point loss can be severe enough to actually set a character back a level, so it's not uncommon to joyously level up only to sadly level back down again after a death. But falling more than a single level is almost unheard of.

Pets are a good way of staving off death in the game because they can be sent out to die in place of the player. Pets — beagles, German shepherds, and wolves, for example — are gained by beating the wild animal as it attacks you and then, when its health is low, feeding it a steak before it kills you or you kill it. You can have more than one pet with you as your roam the countryside and you can kennel them when they're not needed.

Official quests are assigned when your characters reach levels 15, 30, and 45. The format of the quest (what you do, whom you visit, and what you earn for successful completion of the quest) depends on your class. Wizards earn magical gear or skills for their quest. Knights earn armor. Elves earn assorted items. And princes/princesses earn royal cloaks and other paraphernalia of nobility.

You can be officially married in this game as well, and getting hitched will allow you to use your wedding ring to teleport to your spouse whenever you like. The wedding itself must be conducted inside the cathedral and no same-sex marriages or multiple marriages are allowed. But there is also divorce in this game, so if both players agree to the annulment they can both remarry.

Guilds are formed through "blood pledges" that can be initiated only by princes and princesses. Once the pledge group is assembled they can purchase a pledge house through auction or lay siege to one of the castles that are owned and have to be defended by other pledge groups. An invading group can then capture a castle by killing the prince who owns it, stealing his crown from deep inside the guardian tower, or forcing the resident prince to surrender. In this kind of situation, then, the life of the royal character becomes far more important than the lives of the other pledge members — who can be killed without jeopardizing the ownership of the castle.

Larger alliances can be formed, however, in which princes give up all of their leadership abilities to swear to another royal (who then takes "possession" of the lower prince's pledge members). This is how large armies are formed inside the game.

With player-killing, siege warfare, and a feudal hierarchy, this is a game that is not likely to appeal to folks with a democratic mindset or a peaceful or independent spirit. But it is likely to appeal to those who enjoy king-of-the-castle style games and low-pixel-count, low-frame-rate, strategy-game-style isometric graphics.

Star Wars Galaxies:

(starwarsgalaxies.station.sony.com)

The most interesting features of *Star Wars Galaxies* include:

- an enormous lore to draw upon
- macros, in-game auctions, and an entertainer profession used to heal psychic wounds
- a pet system that allows you to capture and create baby creatures and watch them grow (and fight for you)
- and the chance to become a Jedi.

Star Wars Galaxies, from LucasArts and Sony Online Entertainment, is different from most existing MMORPGs in that it has an enormous existing lore — called "the canon" by the developers — to which the game's landscapes, characters, and plot structure must remain faithful. Great care has been taken to keep the basic look and feel of the game true to that of the movies while allowing some room for an expanded vision.

The game takes place at the time of the first Death Star's destruction during the Galactic Civil War. And there are "theme parks" within the game that allow players to encounter characters from the original movie trilogy, including places like the Emperor's Retreat, Jabba's Palace, and various Rebel hideouts. Once players have "earned" entrance into one of these parks, they can have a "narrative experience" and can go off on missions assigned by the theme park residents.

There are ten planets to explore, including Tatooine and Naboo. And none of the planets is completely dominated by one faction or the other, though some planets have a greater Imperial or Rebel presence. And travel between the planets is direct in the initial game (leave one world, enter the next). But space travel itself will be allowed in the future expansions.

You have eight species to choose from for your character. These include Humans, Wookiees, Rodians, Twi'lek, Zabrak, Bothan, Mon Calamari, and Trandoshan. You cannot play any of the main protagonists from the movies (Leia, Luke, etc.), but you can ally yourself with either the Imperial forces or the Rebels (or remain neutral). And you can also write a short autobiography for your character that can be seen by other players.

Characters do not level in this game. So there is not one form of XP that players earn by bonking monsters and spreading the resulting XP among their various skills. Instead, the successful use of a particular skill grants the player XP that is unique to that skill type (surveying XP, animal training XP, or pistol XP, for example).

You have 33 professions to choose from and all of them have typical skills associated with them which are arranged into a skill tree. (There are about 600 skills altogether.) You have to master the lower level skills before being able to tackle the higher level ones. But you can take up more than one profession at a time (currently the limit is four) and some professions require you to develop skills in other professions first. (You can also abandon skills to provide room for others, but you don't regain the skill credits or XP that went into acquiring those skills.)

The skill tree is very extensive and the path of specialization begins early, so the best approach is to figure out what kind of character you want to eventually develop into, and then to aim for those skills right from the start. Each race has some slight innate strengths. Twi'leks, for example, are natural entertainers. Trandoshans, with higher melee defense, are natural unarmed fighters. And Wookiees, are slightly better at creature taming. So, if you know you want to work with monster pets exclusively, for example, you might first create a Wookiee character and then choose Scout as your starting profession. Mastering Hunting and Exploration in this profession would then allow you to take on the Elite Profession of Creature Handler.

Starting professions include Artisan, Brawler, Entertainer, Scout, Marksman, and Medic. And each of these leads to a different group of Elite Professions such as Architect, Fencer, Image Designer (able to change another character's appearance), Ranger, Rifleman, or Doctor. There are hybrid Elite Professions as well that require skills from more than one path. Bioengineer, for example, requires both Scout and Medic expertise, and Bounty Hunter requires mastery of both Scout and Marksman professions.

Combat is done with both range weapons and hand-to-hand weapons (including lightsabers). And for the range weapons your stance (prone, kneeling, standing) affects your aim/accuracy and vulnerability to attack.

But there are different levels of damage in this world and two levels of "death." If any of your three primary attributes — Health, Action (stamina), or Mind (mental health) — are reduced to zero by attacks, you'll fall to the ground, incapacitated. But you won't die unless the creature then decides to deliver a Death Blow. If he backs off, you simply wait on the ground for your attributes to recover and then go about your business. (Three knockdowns in ten minutes, however, will cause you to die).

You can suffer not only temporary reductions to your attributes in a fight but also "wounds" and "battle fatigue" which you cannot heal on your own. The wounds lower your maximum attributes and are healed by those in the doctoring and entertaining professions. Doctors and Medics with stimpacks and medicines heal Health. But psychic wounds and battle fatigue (from too much fighting) are healed by players of the Entertainer profession who dance and play in the town cantinas.

If you die, you return to life at the Cloning Facility you registered at before embarking on your journey. And if you insured your goods beforehand, they reincarnate with you. Otherwise, you'll have to fetch them from the corpse, perhaps with the help of another player whom you can permit to drag your body to a safe area.

When you croak a creature you can harvest resources from it (bone or hide, for example) and you can create macros (such as "/loot;/harvest") that speed up this process.

These macros are also useful in crafting. And craft skills include all the usual suspects, although in this game they are elevated to the level of professions. Armorsmith, tailor, architect, bioengineer, chef, droid engineer, and weaponsmith all use schematics to build higher-level objects.

Crafts and loot can be sold in the Bazaar, the in-game retail and auction system that allows you to place items you want to sell on a board along with your price or minimum accepted bid (in game money) and a time period for selling. When the sale is made, your bank account is added to. If you like, you can also build a shop and sell your wares from it directly.

Quests, called Missions, are generally geared toward the profession of the player, so there are Crafting quests as well as Bounty Hunting, Surveying, and Entertainment quests along with the usual Destroy and

Delivery missions. Random mission terminals are located in the cities. And some quests require a bond — money that the player puts up at the start of the mission. When the mission is successfully concluded, that bond is returned and the reward is granted. If the mission fails, however, the player loses the bond and may end up with a bounty placed on his own head.

Having a bounty assigned to you is one way to be tossed into the PvP [player versus player] system. Other ways of going PK include consensual dueling with one or more players, factional fighting between Imperial or Rebel allies, battlefield wars, and declared hostilities between guilds (called Player Associations). Because there are no levels for characters and because players who are facing off against each other are not allowed to "consider" (study the skill and ability levels) of the character they're fighting, low-level characters shouldn't have to run in terror from bullies as they do in many PK worlds.

Friendship and interaction are encouraged in the game. In fact, there are some game engine mechanisms that make it necessary. Some professions (Bounty Hunter, for example) require that the player take on an apprentice (teach skills to another player) before being allowed to progress in skill development. And some actions (camp-building by a Scout, for instance) can benefit other players in a gang (although with two or more Scouts or Doctors in a group, competition can erupt over which ones will do the healing and harvesting to gain XP). Players who are officially grouped together can communicate within the group and can even automatically follow another group member by clicking "follow" from the other player's menu.

There are also some interesting added touches in the game. A built-in alarm clock allows players to warn themselves about events in the real world or to set time limits on their own play. Characters are given a certain number of building lots on which they can construct their own domiciles. And you can own both pets (some of them quite enormous) as well as droids in the game. To acquire a pet, you first have to tame a baby creature, then train it, and as the pet grows, it can learn to respond to your commands. But you have to both heal it while it's fighting and play with it after battle (to improve its mental health) if you want it to grow up into an adult animal.

The lore of this game will certainly attract large numbers of players. But its flexibility will also attract people. Effort has been expended to make the game fully playable by individuals acting on their own while putting in features that encourage group play. And, unlike in warring clan games, non-violent solo players here have the chance to advance just as fast and far as players who band together or turn PK.

Middle Earth Online:
(www.middle-earthonline.com)

> Middle Earth Online's unique features include:
>
> - the setting, scenery, and ethos of Tolkien's Lord of the Rings novels
> - a built-in automation system (similar to macroing) that allows players to execute some of their in-game actions while offline
> - and a "private encounter" system that reduces camping by creating some quest dungeons and areas that are enterable only by single players or fellowships.

In *Middle Earth Online*, from Turbine Engineering, you have the chance to play either a human, an elf, a hobbit, or a dwarf in a landscape that features the famous locations from the Lord of the Rings novels (including Moria, Bree, Rivendell, and the Shire), the lesser-known localities (such as the icy northern Forochel; green Lindon on the shores west of the Blue Mountains; Angmar, realm of the Witch-king), and, eventually, areas mentioned in *The Hobbit* (such as Mirkwood and Lonely Mountain).

The game takes place just after Frodo and the Fellowship exit the mines of Moria (near the end of the first book). And, because the player characters are all allied races, true player vs. player combat would not make sense and will not be allowed.

You're not restricted, however, to playing on the side of goodness and light in this world. You may just as easily play on the side of Sauron's forces of chaos as on behalf of Gandalf's forces of good. But your decisions affect how other players and NPCs respond to you. Every action will push your character in one direction along the spectrum of valor or corruption, eventually marking it as good or evil and determining its friends and enemies among the game's residents. (Don't expect to be welcomed into Hobbiton, for example, if you're a confederate of the Nazgûl.) Even quest outcomes in this game are influenced by the decisions that players make to push their moral alignment in one direction or the other.

Gameplay is facilitated in interesting ways. First, players can set up tasks for their characters to perform while the player is offline. This is a way of making macroing part of the game itself, and makes leveling easier for casual players while allowing fanatical players to get ahead even while their physical bodies are asleep. Second, some quest dungeons and areas are specially created on the fly by the game engine and prevent entry by anyone but a single player or that player's fellowship. This makes questing a more individualized endeavor and keeps others from camping for a popular quest item or treasure spot.

The classes revolve around adventuring (fighting), exploring, and crafting; and the race you select influences the abilities and skill choices of your character.

There are several methods of transportation beyond walking (boats and wagons, for example). And there are multiple levels of housing for both individuals and guilds (called "kinships"), everything from comfy hobbit holes to elegant mansions. Players, however, cannot build their own houses. They must buy and occupy existing houses created by the developers.

Most players are likely to play the game for the experience of living in the realm of Middle Earth and feeling part of the fictional setting, and this is clearly the game's principle allure. But the game's innovative features are also likely to attract long-time MMORPG players.

Other games to look for:

D&D Online—A world based on the layout and ruleset of the 3.5 edition of Dungeons & Dragons, it emphasizes small groups (a few hundred) in each world to maximize the sense of accomplishment.

Endless Ages—The tie-dyed shirt of the MMORPG world, psychedelic and interesting, created by a small developer group.

Final Fantasy XI—The first MMORPG version of the incredibly long-lived Final Fantasy franchise features linked skill chains for battle, mounts (chocobos, ferries, airships), missions, crystal synthesis, and conquest.

Horizons— Flying characters (dragons), building and town construction, and a school-based skill system with portal construction as a trade skill. Cable modem recommended.

Matrix Online— Allows both Bullet Time and Wire Fu.

Pirates of the Burning Sea— Broadband required. Play a sea captain on the eighteenth century Caribbean.

Ragnarok Online— Isometric view game very popular with kids in Asia.

Rubies of Eventide—Slow zone changes and lag on a modem, but has everything a medieval fantasy world should have. Small group of developers. Modified turn-based fighting.

Second Life— Broadband required. For those looking for creative play without the violence, allows players to be, essentially, developers of the game world.

World of Warcraft—MMORPG version for players of the popular original WoW series.

Chapter 6

The Private World
of MMORPGs

*"There is only one admirable form of the imagination: the imagination
that is so intense that it creates a new reality...."*
— Sean O'Faolain

*"Technology is a way of organizing the universe so that man doesn't have
to experience it."*
— Max Frisch

Each MMORPG is a separate universe. And much of what makes
each one unique is created by the players themselves. Each world, for
example, develops its own dialect, its own shortcuts, and its own spin-
offs. And the players who enrich their world by adding the innumer-
able elements that go into forming its culture often put thousands of
hours of their own time into creating their game society's traditions,
language, customs, and way of life.

Spawned Enterprises: Go Forth and Multiply

One particularly rich aspect of player-created global MMORPG
culture has to do with the spin-offs players produce to supplement the
game worlds themselves.

If a player has trouble understanding the directions to a quest, for
example, or figuring out how to cast a ring spell, or is stuck in the badlands with no idea of where to run, help is always available in the form

of Web sites established or contributed to by fellow players who are so interested in the game that they put their own encyclopedic knowledge and programming skills to use for the benefit of newbies.

These repositories of arcane and abstruse information have come to fill a valuable niche in every game. In fact, much of the allure of any game is actually located outside of the game itself in separate sites scattered around the net. And for the millions of players who use these information sites, they constitute an invaluable addition to the culture of the game.

Fan sites — created or supplemented by players — offer the chance to find advice, information, and camaraderie with other players. They are written for the benefit of both newbies and advanced players. And they're generally up-to-the-minute in their data and recommendations. They stay this way, typically, because players who make discoveries in the game contribute their knowledge to the site so that everyone can share in the bounty. Fan sites run the gamut from small and simple to huge and complex. At the lower end are one-page Everything You Ever Wanted to Know FAQs that fill novices in on the practical matters of how to acquire a particular quest item or how to cook plants to make armor dye. At the more obsessive end are five-thousand-item searchable databases filled with spoilers — complete information on every aspect of game play that players would otherwise have to discover for themselves by trial and error inside the game.

After you've typed the name of your particular MMORPG into any general search engine to find the fan sites you need, you'll see that most of them divide up their information according to the same general categories.

- There is always a bestiary that shows the creatures in the game, including their skill levels, their strengths and weaknesses, and their typical locations, so you can determine ahead of time where, what, and how you would like to hunt.
- There's a cartography section with maps to every dungeon and outdoor location.
- There are shop lists of vendors that include their locations, the items they sell, and sometimes the rates at which they deal in their commodities ("This vendor buys clothing at 80% of its listed value and sells at 120%").

- There are laundry lists of the items it is possible to buy, items it is possible to make, and items that can be found in quests.
- There are libraries that contain every printed word spoken by every quest-initiating NPC in the game, along with the histories of the various races, and compendia of planetary political documents.
- There are guides to all of the professions and trade skills allowed in the game, complete with the success and failure rates of different crafting endeavors arranged by level ("Those with lock-picking skills under 125 will fail 80% of the time in making this key").
- And there are recipes for foods, alchemical preparations, and magical spells, including the order in which the ingredients have to be mixed together and their resulting effects on the body.

From these fan sites there are also pointers to other Web sites that feature subsidiary programs — plug-ins created by fanatical players who are also programmers. These addenda are often not officially endorsed by the game's developers. In fact, sometimes they're not allowed — being seen as violations of the player licensing agreement. But they are so undeniably useful that they're irresistible to hardcore players.

Interactive maps are one popular plug-in. They allow a player to type their character's coordinates into the map and then see and study the neighboring surroundings in a far greater depth than is possible with the official map in the game's GUI. Some interactive maps even allow players to upload a running commentary attached to any location so that others who download the map can read a fellow explorer's narrative of what they should expect to see and experience at certain coordinates.

Macro development kits are also popular subsidiary applications. They can add the flavor of a strategy game to the MMORPG world because they allow you to act as the manager of your character, as if the character were a serf being assigned to mine gold or cut wood while you're away. Players can come back at the end of eight hours of work or sleep to find their packs stuffed with coins and their macro-directed characters stuffed with experience points.

A more invasive form of program that takes control of your game's interface, called an "augmenter," is also available on spin-off sites. One type of augmenter called a "revealer," for example, places a new window in your game panel that allows you to identify all loot above a certain value dropped on the ground near you. Where you might once have merrily tread past millions of valuable goodies without even knowing they were there, this kind of application highlights the presence of the objects as you run by them. Sometimes you can set the program to search out particular creatures you're interested in hunting and beep you when such creatures appear in the neighborhood. You may also be able to set the revealer to trigger an alert when one of your friends (or enemies if you're a player-killer) wanders nearby.

This extrasensory perception is so helpful to the players who use it that tools like this are often banned by the official developers because they unbalance the game. They give an unfair advantage to the players who use them. However, once people try them, they're often hooked and there's usually no way the developers can tell that someone is running an augmenting program on their home machine. So, such useful programs tend to spread like viruses. And no one seems to feel any guilt about using them because they usually perform functions that the developers should have included in the game in the first place. Common augmenters include profanity filters, real-time chat logs, and shortest path calculators.

There are some kinds of augmentation, however, that can be detected by people inside the game. One is the "state preserver" program. Such a program allows players to capture a given state in the game — say, a particular animation sequence designed by the developers — and to then use it in ways that it was not intended to be used. A character may, for example, walk around in the game looking as if it is about to evaporate from the landscape.

Another type of augmenter can jimmy the speed control of a character. Running this program allows the character to travel at two or three times the speed of the fastest thing in the game. Often though, this sucks up so many CPU cycles from the server that it lags everyone else in the vicinity. And that leads to the person being reported and, sometimes, excommunicated from the game. So, this is a program that is best run only in the middle of the desert or out in empty space away from other players.

The number of auxiliary programs always grows as a game's popularity grows. So, once the game has more than 50,000 players, there are likely to be dozens of third-party plug-ins available, including:

- a program that translates written chat conversations into audible speech
- one that gives the relative location of all of the player-killers on your enemies list
- a real-time social directory that lists everyone in your circle of friends along with their current level, location, and presence online
- a live list of all the places whose coordinates you want to remember
- a program that selects and plays background music (from a playlist of wavs or MP3s that you provide) according to the type of activity you're engaging in (battling, shopping, chatting, etc.)
- a plug-in that allows you to simply click on buttons listing all possible physical emotes (play dead, jump for joy, scold, beg for mercy ...) so you can perform them with a key click instead of having to remember and type in the specific and often complicated names for each
- real estate management programs for players who build or buy property in the game
- business management programs for people who maintain tradebots selling their manufactured goods to other players
- skins that replace the existing game GUI with other graphics
- quest management systems that allow you to create, flowchart, and distribute your own quests inside the game
- sorting programs to arrange all of your character's loot, weapons, and spell components
- and programs to set up a temporary system of player-killing for non-player-killer games or for players who want to try out player-killing briefly.

In addition to all of this code generated by players, many people also write stories based on their own characters or on the setting of the world they're playing in. This work is stored on fan fiction sites scattered around the net. And it's a completely natural outgrowth of game life for most people because a huge number of MMORPG players are also fantasy fiction readers looking for ways to surround themselves with the worlds in their imaginations.

Writing fan fiction is always a labor of love. It allows players to immerse themselves in the characters, plot, and *genius loci* of a particular realm and time period. And if the game servers are down, people sometimes turn to the fiction sites to get their "fix" of their imaginary universe. Or they print out the stories and read them when they're at work or school.

No one writes these tales to become famous or to make money. There's no money involved. And there's no fame. In fact, most people who contribute stories to fan sites usually sign the story with their game name, not their real name. They write because the process of writing helps them visualize their virtual lives and makes the game experience even richer.

In fact, the extraordinary thing about most MMORPGs is that, for every hour the game's official developers put into creating the game, the players themselves collectively put in another three or four hours enhancing and expanding upon the developers' vision and the game's functionality. And now that MMORPG game development code is going open source, this kind of collaborative work is likely to skyrocket.

Macros and Bots and Scripts, Oh My

The second activity spun off by MMORPG players is the use of small computer programs that guide the actions of characters — shortcuts that take the form of macros. These are lists of mouse positions, cursor movements, calculations, and key clicks that are run while the player is doing something else in the real world. And, to activate them, a player presses a single button to run all of the commands in the list. The instructions are then executed by the game character in sequence.

Most people who are familiar with macros in their word processing or spreadsheet applications think of them as five- or six-line programs tied to the "hot keys" (F1 through F12) at the top of their keyboard. But macros can do much more than execute a few equations. In a MMORPG game, they can give a character a life separate from that of the player.

They can direct a character's movements and actions for hours at a time while making money and gaining experience inside the game — all without the player physically monitoring what's happening on the screen.

Macro-development tools are usually created by people not affiliated with a game company — programmers who happen to love a particular game and see a way to speed up the repetitive parts of it. But the script that is loaded into the tool and executes the tasks to be followed by the character is written by the individual players, so some coding experience can be helpful in creating macros (this is also a good way for kids to learn some elements of programming).

Macros automate the processes that are most time-consuming in a game, including mage spellcasting, hack-and-slash combat, the trading of manufactured goods, scavenging for dropped loot, and every trade skill from cooking and fletching to alchemy and tinkering. Using command sequences that sometimes number in the thousands of lines, these macros eventually become "bots" — characters that move and act independently of the player's control.

When my daughter, Bunyip, for example, complained that her character never had enough money to buy all the sundresses, lounging robes, and wedding gowns she "needed," I decided to build her a bot. I thought of a "litter picker" to scavenge the countryside for abandoned loot; a "wall-licker," a mage that drains the life out of creatures all day while hiding in caves to avoid attack; a "buff bot" that could stand outside a well-populated dungeon and cast beneficial spells (buffs) on people entering to fight; a "portalbot" that could stand in the middle of town and offer people wormhole trips to destinations on the outer edges of the game world; and a fletcher to make and sell arrows. But I settled on a bot whose only purpose was to stand outside the grocery shop and make fish pies all day.

The macro script I wrote controlled a character named Simple Simon who prepared a hundred pies at a time and cashed them in for three times what he had paid for the raw ingredients. He was a slow bot, but that didn't matter because I didn't have to be with the character while he was doing his job. And after only a few days of work, he had accumulated 50,000 coins — enough for several dresses for my daughter's character.

His construction was rather simple, consisting mostly of commands like "MousePos 760, 360" to bring the cursor over the first slot in his backpack, followed by "LEFTCLICK" to select the water there, and then "Keys 9" to choose the dough-making task from my hotpanel (also called a quickbar — the spot on the interface where you put icons that actuate the tasks you want to do all the time). I only had to throw in a "Loop 100" command and a few dozen other commands to control the cutting of fish, the stacking of items, and the buying of new supplies, and 100 pies at a time were made while I did other things.

In this case, I set the program to beep me when the pies were sold, but the one problem with most game macros is that there's no way to receive feedback from the game itself or to respond to unexpected changes. So, if you construct a combat bot and program it to roam the landscape croaking golems, for example, it may not be able to tell you that it has died.

This is a big problem with combat bots that roam the land gaining experience on their own. They sometimes die in the first five minutes of battling, losing all of their armor, and then die over and over again until the landscape is strewn with dozens of loincloth-clad corpses, all while the player is off having a snack. When the player returns his character has no possessions and has a sizeable death penalty to work off.

Sadly, not all games allow macros to exist because some developers regard them as exploits. And the games that don't tolerate macroing may even go so far as to run diagnostic scans of character behavior to check for robotic play, or to send private messages to characters just to see if the player is at the keyboard controlling the character. The penalty for getting caught is usually temporary or permanent banishment from the game.

Most of the players I interviewed, however, believed that macros enriched the game experience enormously. Many considered them to be the most interesting and technically challenging part of any game. So, as the next generation of games is developed, developers are likely to not only allow the practice but even facilitate it with macroing tools and ready-made scripts built into the game.

Slang: Who You Callin' a Twinked Noob

The third and most obvious players' contribution in the realm of spin-offs is in the area of language.

People speak such a strange patois in MMORPG worlds and at LAN-parties (where groups of people get together in one room to play an online game) that it's common for new players to flounder in confusion for a few days trying to sort out what everyone is saying. In fact, conversations often take on a surreal cast in the beginning.

A typical conversation might go:

"This char's so gimped, it needs major loving even twinked n buffed!"

"Lol. Between mob aggro and pk gankfests, there's no phat lewt left on me!"

"Omg! Griefing as a trade skill! w00t! rotglmao!"

"What's the emote for wtf?"

"Rogl, such a noob."

"That's ubernoob to u, m8. Could be a perching mage tank if they'd quit with the nerf patches, rollbacks, lag beast, and server drops. Need to learn the exploit for deathlessness."

"No. You just have to learn to summon pets, mount up, and portal out before the debuffs hit, then you're not lugging that death penalty burden around."

This slang is not an affectation. It's actually quite necessary because game life is so larded with unique experiences, inside jokes, and tech jargon that it requires a new language to describe it all. It's a concise language that emphasizes shorthand, abbreviation, and linguistic economy. And, over time, most players adopt the speech patterns of the game they're in, becoming genuine citizens of the virtual world.

When interpreting MMORPG-speak, think first of brevity.

The spelling of many phrases, for example, is done in chat room rebus fashion to save on keystrokes. "Anyone" becomes "nel." And "g2g" is "got to go." Most single words are similarly contracted. "Are" becomes "r." "And" becomes just "n." Both "him" and "them" become "m." And "okay" becomes "k."

Many multiword phrases are reduced to acronyms. "RL" refers to "real life." "Brb" means "Be right back." "Btw" is "by the way." "Omg" is "oh, my god." "Nm" is "never mind." "Afk" is "away from keyboard." "IMHO" is "in my humble opinion" (usually capitalized, which is strange if you're trying to connote humility). "Ty" is "thank you." "Mt" is "many thanks." "Np" is "no problem." "See you later" becomes "cya." "Pc" is "price check"—a request for people nearby to tell you how much an object you just found is worth. "Iso" is "in search of"—a way of letting other players know that you're on the prowl for a particular item. "Woot!" or "w00t!" are expressions of joyful triumph. And the ubiquitous "lol" means "laugh out loud." Its extensions include "rogl" (rolling on ground laughing) and "rotglmao" (rolling on the ground laughing my ass off).

The F word—or, actually, just the F, not the whole word—is sprinkled into game speak anywhere emphasis is required. "Wtf" is "what the …"—an expression used by players who are deeply puzzled. And "omfg," "rotglmfao," and "nfp" are all used for humorous effect.

Some words are simply contracted. A "noob" is a "newbie"—a term of ridicule for some, an admission of innocence for others. After a while in the game you rise to the level of a "lowbie." "Character" becomes "char." Another word for a character is "toon," from "cartoon." "Probably" becomes "prolly." "Decomposed" is "decomped." And "lewt," or "loot," is both a noun (describing what you collect from a corpse) and a verb (the act of raiding cadavers).

The same concision occurs in all of the real languages that people use in the game world (the most common being French, Swedish, Danish, Korean, German, Japanese, and Dutch). Francophones, for example, often use "pkoi" instead of "pourquoi" to save a few keystrokes. "Quebecois" becomes "kebekoi." "Qu'est-ce que c'est" becomes "kes k c." When I roamed around the game world in the morning, looking for my corpses, saying, "Un autre jour, un autre corps" (another day, another body) I'd sometimes hear back "r)" (rire: to laugh) from the guys playing simultaneously in the suburbs of Paris.

The one borrowed foreign word used by all players is "uber"—from the German word for "over" or "above" (as in the national anthem: *Deutschland über alles*). Uber in the game context refers to very high-level items that can be attained only by powerful characters or large groups working together.

Many words refer to ideas unique to MMORPG life. "Level," for example, means rising up a notch in the hierarchy of game characters. "Trade skills" refer to the nonviolent ways of gaining experience — everything from cooking to blacksmithing to singing. "Emotes" are the physical gestures and postures that characters perform after the player types, for example, "dance," "beg," or "YMCA." "Portals" are the wormholes that lead to other parts of a world's landscape. And "retired" items are those no longer being found as loot or treasure anywhere in the game world. These are often the rarest and most valuable items in the game.

Some words refer to the mechanics of the world itself. "Exploits," for example, are the schemes or techniques that savvy (or dishonest) players use to gain something without working very hard for it, often taking advantage of bugs in the game engine code to make big money or level up. Sometimes game developers will find out about an exploit quickly and will rollback the databases to undo its effects. During such a "rollback" a company resets all characters on a server back to their levels of the previous day, wiping out all the experience and loot they'd gained in the last 24 hours. Rollbacks are intensely annoying to the players, so they're only done in emergencies.

"Lag," however, is a common annoyance. Lag is the jitter and jerky movement that happens when the rendering engine can't draw images on the screen fast enough. And it's sometimes a prelude to "server drop" — the cutting of the link between a home computer and the company's server. When the connection drops, your character usually remains exactly where it was in the virtual landscape. If this is in the middle of a monster "spawn," your character will probably be killed while you are offline. Then you'll reconnect to the game later, only to find yourself reincarnated somewhere else while your cadaver rots in the spot you were in when the connection dropped. Sometimes when this happens you end up in a different zone completely. "Zones" are the sections of a game world that require the loading of files onto your computer when you enter them.

A great deal of game slang refers to the exercise of power in the virtual world.

One of the things, for example, that an advanced character can do for a lower-level character is to "tank" for him or her. A tank is a high-level character who acts as a decoy for monsters (monsters are called "mobs" in some games). The tank stands openly in defiance of their attacks while a lower-level character pecks at the creatures and gains experience points. When the low-level character is pounced upon by the monsters, the tank then heals the lower-level character so it can continue fighting. This kind of arrangement is a way for one character to help another character "power-level" (grow quickly).

Another way to help a lower-level character is through "twinking." A "twinked" character is one whose abilities have been temporarily boosted in some way, allowing it to do things and go places that would not ordinarily be within its powers. Twinking might be accomplished by giving an uber-saber to a lowbie sword-swinger. Or it might require casting an invulnerability spell on a weak newbie. This latter act is known as "buffing"— strengthening a character or temporarily improving its abilities through magic (or through technology in a sci-fi game).

"De-buffing" and "nerfing" refer to the opposite effects. De-buffs are disabling or enervating spells usually cast by monsters on characters. Once weakened by the de-buff, a character may fall easy prey to the monster's specific attack mechanism.

"Nerfing" is the lowering of a weapon's power, the weakening of armor's protective ability, or the reduction of a character's power by the game developers. This is done because developers strive always to maintain a balance between the different professions so that archers or galactic explorers don't zoom easily up to level 50 while the poor mages and planetary traders languish at level 3. One way to achieve this balance is for the developers to give "loving" to a character type that seems weaker than the others (to boost its abilities or give it more powerful skills). Another way is to keep the weapons and armor of the various professions evenly matched. When a new item is created that throws the balance off— conveying to its user so much power that it puts everyone else at a disadvantage — that item has to be nerfed in the next patch. (The "patch" is the occasional update to the game that fixes past bugs, adds new items and quests, and adjusts the scenery of the game.)

Some power words are redefined street slang. One of these is "gimpy," the old vernacular for lameness. Since characters in MMORPG games don't limp, the word is used to designate a character that is not quite up to snuff, a character that is flawed or hampered in some way because of errors in its creation or development made by the player.

Often a player's first character will be severely gimped — able to do many things, but none of them very well. This is usually the result of bad initial design by the player. But sometimes characters are gimped when players change their minds about a character after playing it for a while. Someone who, for example, starts out with the idea of making a sword-wielding character may give that character enormous strength but few magical abilities. If the player then finds magic more fun than monster chopping, all the accumulated future experience points will go into growing that character into a mage. But, because of the early decisions made on its skills and abilities, the character will always be a gimpy mage, one that is less able to perform than characters who were designed from the start with sorcery in mind.

A gimpy character in a player-killer game has to worry about being "ganked." Derived from the phrase "gang up on and kill," ganking is what player-killers do when they ambush a weaker player en masse and beat him to death. Such a hapless player may be able, however, to "charm" or "summon" a monster from the surrounding countryside to help battle his foes. Some charmed creatures are "mounts" that can be ridden. Others act as "pets" capable of defending their masters. And some games even allow you to "morph" into one of the creatures in the landscape yourself — taking on the skills, strengths, and abilities of that species in the process.

Some game slang refers to physical actions taken by players or to physical places inside the game world.

"Perches," for example, are objects that players can jump onto but which are inaccessible to monsters. They are of no use to "melee" characters who have to actually approach the creatures and mix it up with them, but they're useful for archers and mages and anyone who can shoot from a distance. (Creatures that do not "drain" their attackers — suck the health out of them — are the preferred targets.) A character simply finds a spot on the top of a rock pile, up in a tree, or on the roof of a building, and lobs icicles or scorching arrows at the monsters who charge but cannot do any damage because they can't jump up onto the perch.

When the monsters are too far away to reach from the perch,

someone in a group may volunteer to "drag" or "pull" the monsters. "Dragging" (called "train-pulling" or "training" in some games) requires approaching creatures and provoking them into chasing you. "Pulling" means throwing something at the creatures or casting a spell on them to encourage them to chase you.

To do this, players go to a spot where they know a "spawn" of monsters will be available for pulling. A spawn is a group of monsters that always appear together in one area (and reappear together if they're killed).

In most games, spawns of creatures of specific levels reside in particular areas around the game world. You then travel to those areas in search of monsters if you're in the mood for a fight (or you avoid those areas if you've been weakened by attacks or don't have your armor on).

Because spawns are generally predictable, some characters choose to remain in an area for a long period of time to prey on the resident monsters, an activity known as "camping." Oftentimes the characters will camp an area until they've gleaned the "quest item" they were looking for, or have "leveled."

The benefit of camping is that there are usually other characters nearby to help if you get into trouble, and you'll know exactly where your body is when you die. The problem with camping, however, is that you may never get the chance to take on monsters when there are 10 other characters around you all waiting for the next creature to respawn.

This kind of experience can be the source of "griefing" in a game. A "griefer" or "grief player" is — in some games — a player who just enjoys annoying other players and causing them grief. But in most games, a grief player is someone who exposes his own grief on a regular basis, constantly importuning other players for buffs, money, armor, portal jumps, or body retrieval assistance. It may also refer to a character who is always complaining to the game's administrators about other people's camping or kill-stealing, or about being robbed or attacked or mistreated in the game. It's different from "agro," which refers to aggravation, anger, or aggression, usually from monsters or other players.

What happens when you die depends on the world you're in. Your body always drops to the ground. But after that, the game determines your fate. In some games you become a "ghost" and have to make your way back to a "revival terminal." In others you pop back to the "life-stone," "recall point," or "bind point" that you chose earlier. You usually suffer a "death penalty" at this point, losing experience points or leaving a portion of your loot on your body. But it's almost always possible to retrieve your goods and regain your points through diligence and persistence.

Making a MMORPG

If you're considering building a MMORPG or mMORPG (minimally multi-player game), be prepared for an impressively steep learning curve. Developing the skills to create 3D models, animate creatures, lay out complicated game designs, build and populate a landscape, and wrestle with network protocols can take years of diligent effort.

Suitable game engines such as the Torque Engine from Garage Games, or one of the open source engines — Cube 3D, Crystalspace, NeL, and World Forge — are available over the net. And the necessary tools for model development and unwrapping (Milkshape), level-editing/dungeon-building (QuArk, Worldcraft), and version control (Win Cvs, MacCvs) are there as well. But it can take many months to master the programming in any game development package.

Once you have the skills you need, it can take more years to actually build the game — even with lots of friends working on it. This is why both MMORPGs and mMORPGs are developed by groups of specialists in the fields of art, programming, and design. Even in the non-corporate world where one person may wear many hats, the tasks involved in creating a game are usually divided into these three areas.

Game Design

In a big shop, when the game experience is no more than an idea, the creative director and lead designer sit down to flesh out the features to be included in the game. These can be as large as:

- the lore that explains the history of players and creatures in the new game world
- the races available to players
- the overall game economy
- the XP system
- the skills and abilities available to characters
- the dungeons, traps, puzzles, and creature spawn placements
- how quests will work in the game
- and whether and where player-killing will be allowed.

But, beyond these larger issues, there are also thousands of smaller details to worry about, for example:

- the number of experience points that specific creatures will convey
- how quickly corpses will decompose
- the rarity and value of items in the game
- the difficulty of surviving in each area of the landscape
- the length of time that an irritated monster will chase a character
- and what will happen to a character when it jumps off a cliff or eats a banana cream pie.

Once these features are installed, they then have to be balanced— a task that requires thousands of hours of patient testing. If, for example, a mage needs 10 expensive components to cast one spell, but a swordsman can use the same cheap saber over and over, does that make the game much harder for the mages who have to continuously buy spell components? Is it unfair? Would allowing the mage's spells to do more damage make the system more equitable or would it give an unfair advantage to the mage?

All of these considerations become part of the game system — the set of rules that governs how all individual elements in the game behave.

The player is presented with three gates offering helpful, destructive, or false spells in the Educational MMORPG and must recognize the kanji characters for "protection," "barrier," and "fake" in order to choose the right one.

These rules establish the protocols for interaction between the players and everything else, laying out the constraints under which characters can move, shoot, band together, trade with or fight each other, overcome obstacles, grow, develop, and die.

Art

As the game design principles take shape, concept artists work with the art director to sketch out different settings that will define the look and feel of the virtual environment. Then artists from various disciplines bring those concepts to life.

Landscape artists, for example, focus on constructing the world itself using a terrain editor. They designate where the mountains will soar, where the hills will flatten out to desert, and where the canyons will meet the ocean.

The landscapes, initially created in wireframe (using webs of glowing lines and angles called "splines" or "meshes"), are then covered by 2D artists with textures (sometimes called "skins" when applied to models of human or monster figures)—flat photographs, paintings, or drawn images that are mapped onto the terrain and the objects in the world.

Some of these textures are applied to huge individual polygons (cliff faces, for example). Some are stretched over many polygons at once to form decals (such as cave entrances). Some are painted over models of buildings, objects, and characters that have been unwrapped (split apart, flattened out, and stretched). But most landscape textures are tiled— duplicated thousands of times over sprawling terrains — to create desert pavement or glassy lake surfaces.

Meanwhile, another group of artists focuses on designing architectural components and laying out the shapes of buildings and the interiors of dungeons. Still others concentrate on item creation. And together they build everything from edifices, furniture, and boulders to jewelry, weapons, and clothing. When they're done, decorators then place the items inside the game interiors and arrange the trees, rocks, and buildings in outdoor settings.

As the world itself is taking shape, 3D character artists focus on character construction using the same brands of modeling software that are employed to create 3D animated movies, cinematic special effects, and amusement park motion-based virtual reality experiences. In some cases, characters are cobbled together from 3D geometric primitives (spheres, cubes, columns, cones, etc.) and then pulled and prodded like taffy into more sophisticated forms by the artist. In other cases, generic digitized models of humans, objects, or animals are tweaked into specific shapes. And, sometimes, very complex characters are built first as actual physical sculptures in clay, plaster, or plasticine. These real-world sculptures, called maquettes, are then scanned with a 3D scanner to capture the intricacies of their shapes.

While this is happening, 2D artists (often with a background in comics illustration or Web design) tackle the layout of the graphical user interface (GUI) which allows players to see the 3D world of characters and monsters through part of the window, while revealing other objects crucial to the welfare of the character, especially:

- the objects carried in the character's inventory
- the catalogue of experience points, skills, and abilities accumulated so far by the character
- maps and radar scopes that help the character travel through the landscape
- the paper doll—the 2D representation of the character dressed up and equipped with jewelry, armor, and handheld items
- and the sensing devices that allow the character to identify monsters and other characters from a distance.

Animation

Once the 3D character models are available in the computer for experimentation, the animators begin to make these "living" characters move by articulating and boning the models.

Articulation involves establishing where the joints will be placed and how the character will bend. It allows a character to retract its elbow when it pulls back a bow and bend at the knees when it squats to pick up loot. Boning involves inserting virtual femurs, tibias, and vertebrae into parts of the model to let the computer know which segments should remain rigid during typical creature movement. Without boning and articulation the character's body might concertina when it sat down or stretch like a rubber band when it reached for an apple.

To animate them, characters are twisted, in the computer, into a series of frozen positions, called keyframes, while the computer fills in the intervening movements, called tweens. The character may be posed first in a standing position, for example, and then squatting. And the computer then interpolates the movements involved on the path from one posture to the other, compiling the movements into groups called fixed action patterns, kinematic sequences, pose-to-pose sequences, or keyframe sequences.

Such patterns can then be stored separately from the objects they work on in a motion library where they become part of the game's behavioral repertoire. The patterns can then be reused by any of the characters and creatures in the game. One pattern may be called, for example, "character dies a histrionic death" and may include the animated actions "character clutches own heart with both hands," "character tosses head back," and "character collapses forward with resounding thud."

Once these behaviors are stabilized in the library, they can be linked in chains and used in different parts of the game. The "character raises arm with object in hand" movement, for example, can be used in the animated sequences "creature hurls rock," "character shows off a new weapon," or "NPC holds up item for appraisal at an in-game auction."

Many of these movement patterns also end up being reused in the game's system of physical emotes. Words such as "-dance-," "-point-," and "-wave-" are translated into movement patterns that the characters go through when a player types in these commands.

Programming

Many of a game's design rules are built into the infrastructure code of the game engine — code that is added in layers, starting with the rules that apply to everything in the game universe and ending with rules that apply to only one type of monster or player in one particular situation.

At the base level are the "naive physics" rules that establish how inanimate objects will act in the virtual world. We know, for example, that a ball released in midair will drop to the ground in the real world and a flung rock will trace a parabolic trajectory through the sky instead of traveling in a straight line. But in the virtual world, if we let go of an object, it stays there suspended in space until we write the code that tells it what to do.

In a large game, these Newtonian rules may vary depending on the venue. Characters residing on a massive planet or those caught in a maelstrom, for example, may struggle with 5G gravity or centripetal force. And characters outside their ships in space or suspended in magic chambers may find no gravity at all. Creating all of these rules is the job of the physics programmers.

At a higher level are the rules used to enliven the monsters in the game, the rules that determine when the creatures will run, attack, lurk, flock, or sneak up on unsuspecting prey. Even before the final physical forms of the creatures are settled upon, these artificial intelligence modules are designed by AI programmers to give the monsters something approaching complex behavior.

When the game is young, the underlying principles of the physics and the AI code are usually written in C++. But as programmers standardize the basic structures of the game engine, they often spend more and more of their time working in an English-like pseudocode called script. And many script modules take the form of heuristics (rules of thumb) embedded into "objects" (blocks of code that fire when an event triggers them).

While the physics and AI are being worked out, the control mechanisms that constrain how players interact inside the game are also coded. Since a huge part of every game involves trading, looting, selling, and buying, this part of the game system is always a high priority. Players may have to click on a vendor to open a window that shows what is offered for sale, for example. They may have to enchant a creature to turn it into a pet. Or they have to use a "voodoo doll command" to hijack control of another player's character. All of these actions are controlled by the programming that establishes which actions are allowable by the players.

Databases and Servers

When the game is eventually fielded, the user interface is linked to all of the game's disparate systems at once. And the interactions between these different parts of the game are far more complex than is evident from just looking at the screen. This is because part of what appears on the user's screen comes from the user's own computer, called the client. And part is sent to the player from the game company's computer, called the server.

When a player sees, for example, four scintillating gems in his inventory, the pictures of those gems are actually stored in the game directory of that player's own computer. But the fact that there are four of them is pulled from the player's character database which may reside thousands of miles away on the game company's server.

In homemade MMORPG games, this becomes even more complicated because the computer of the person who made the game and invites other players into the game world becomes both the server and one of the clients. (In this kind of game, the number of players allowed into the world is usually controlled by the capacity of the pipe carrying the server's signals. A broadband user on a cable modem, for example, may have 64 other players in the world with him. Someone serving up a MMORPG game from a small-bandwidth dial-up system, however, may be allowed only one or two other players.)

In addition to the character database, there are item and creature databases keeping track of the health, value, or whereabouts of hundreds of thousands of separate creatures and items scattered throughout the game world. And these also have to be integrated into the game's GUI.

Story, Sound, and Music

Finally, when the essential design features have been fleshed out, the game engine is working, the databases are populated, and the AI is functioning, the lore that will pull all of the game's action together is inserted. Worked on since the beginning of game development, this backstory lays out the history of the various races, explains what the players' characters are doing in the game world, and establishes the narrative groundwork for future plot twists. Some games even hire fantasy novelists or sci-fi writers to give their lore and episodic updates a polished feel because, for many players, a complex and engaging storyline is crucial to their enjoyment of the game.

The first audio is also likely to appear in the game once all the fundamentals have been worked out. Sound designers search for months for the appropriate sound effects. And it's not unusual for them to walk around banging every pipe and turning on every faucet in hopes of finding a perfect sound for the game. They may sprinkle paper clips on tables to create the clatter of clawed werewolves running down wooden stairs. They may tap coconut halves with pencils to make the sound of rain on the bamboo roof of a hut. They may knock hammers against metal cables to make the clang of flung knives pelting armor. They may yank duct tape to make the sound of a shirt ripping. And they may pull lettuce heads apart to make the sound of tearing flesh.

Music is often inserted at this point in development as well. Game music is usually composed in ostinati (loops) to make it easier to link to the different forms of action within the game. Composers work with programmers at this stage to make sure that certain actions on the character's part or certain areas of the game world trigger the appropriate melodies. Pastoral symphonic preludes come up when you're resting. Suspense/thriller high-strings-over-heartbeats come up when you're stalking prey. And raucous industrial techno makes the speakers rattle when you're battling behemoths. (The problem with these loops is that they sometimes contain too many measures and extend beyond the actions on the screen, so you're still hearing idyllic flutes even after you've started blasting ferocious critters, or you're still listening to heroic trumpets even when the monsters are all dead and you're eating an apple to celebrate.)

Final Touches

Once the game's major components are installed, the first alpha tests are done in-house among the game's developers and their families. And when the game is finally publicly fielded in stages during beta testing, it's the long-distance and multiplayer aspects of the game that get the greatest workout.

The networking code that controls the server/client relationship and the management of packet streams is put through its paces. Then the beta tests gradually take on more and more players to make sure the code can keep thousands of participants connected to the server simultaneously without dropping connections or allowing any latency (lag) between when a button is pressed and when an action is executed on the screen.

At the same time, the graphical component of the game engine, sometimes called the rendering engine, is pushed to handle the rapid realtime redrawing of the world on the user's monitor. This is a formidable task because while objects already exist in the real world before you look at them, objects in the virtual world don't exist until you look at them. If you turn your character to gaze off the edge of a cliff into a forest canopy, the computer has to calculate where you are looking and what it should draw in that spot. It then has to paint that scene in front of you 30 times a second to give you the illusion of an actual landscape. And it does so while maintaining the proper perspective in three dimensions because MMORPG worlds are not like the old flat scrolling video game worlds. They exist on the X (across) and Y (up/down) planes, but they also contain a Z axis (into and out of the screen). As a result, the number of sequential calculations done by the game engine to sort out where you're looking and to draw the images you should see is quite spectacular.

On top of all of this is draped a communications layer that requires its own separate programming designed to allow characters to broadcast messages, chat privately, and send alerts to each other.

When a game draws in more users than can fit on one server (usually about 2,000–4000 concurrent players) a "lobby" system then has to be set up to allow users to choose from among several starting servers.

Finally, in some games, localization is added for players who want all of their in-game instructions in Korean or French or Swedish. And then the game is ready to ship.

When the game goes gold (retails), a smaller group of developers called the live team takes over the updating and enhancement of the game. Because the storyline is extended and new features are added on a continuing basis, their job is never really finished until the replacement version of the game comes along. And often they engage in live ops by entering the game in the guise of a monster or lore character and interacting with the players.

For a large MMORPG, this entire process of game development usually takes one and a half to three years and costs several million dollars. But financial catastrophes, deadline logjams, and organizational meltdowns can add a year or more to the schedule and hundreds of thousands of dollars in expenses to the budget.

The final result, however, may be well worth the investment. Even a game that attracts only 30,000 players — a modest number in the MMORPG world — can bring in $1.5 million through purchase of the game and another $3 million–$5 million per annum from subscriptions. And this does not include the licensing fees that the game development company can charge if it turns its code into generic tools that other game companies can use to build MMORPGs or licenses its characters to merchandisers.

Games generally last three to six years before they are replaced by their own Version 2, so a popular game can generate vast sums of money during its lifetime, not including movie rights, novelizations, or merchandising spin-offs. And some games continue even when they've been officially "replaced" by their Version 2. No one yet knows, in fact, how long some of the early games will last.

Chapter 8

The Future of MMORPGs

"Everything you can imagine is real."— Pablo Picasso

"All men by nature desire knowledge."— Aristotle

Based on the technologies now available and those still evolving, six aspects of the future development of MMORPG games are obvious and inevitable.

First, the quality of the graphics will certainly improve from year to year. The earliest games featured blocky 3D objects, character faces that were nothing more than spheres with decals pulled over them, shoulders that came to a sharp point, and hands that looked like mittens. But the second generation showed a leap forward in the granularity of the images and in the polygon count (the number of flat planes that go into making characters and other 3D objects). This trend toward visual complexity will certainly continue as the technology improves enough to eventually offer cinematic levels of realism.

Second, the sophistication of the AI used in MMORPGs will grow as the games evolve. Creature AI (the programming that controls the behavior of monsters and NPCs) was rather simple in first-generation games, sometimes no more than binary (chase vs. flee, attack vs. stand). But the same trend that occurred in the scientific world as programmers moved from linear programming to object-based and then to subsumptive and emergent programming is occurring in the game world as well.

Instead of featuring monsters that attack every character the same way every time, games will feature monsters that figure out the optimum way in which to attack your particular character. They may blast you first with lightning or with fire. They may hound you through the woods or spring out at you in a box canyon. They may fall on your head from a tree branch or rise out of a tunnel they have dug beneath your feet.

And each time they attack, they'll keep track of how much damage they do to you until they discover your weaknesses — exactly as a player-killer would do. They'll learn from each attack. When they die, they'll catalogue how you managed to kill them. And, when they respawn, it will be with tactics better suited to dealing with your tactics. In time, individual creatures of the same species will even share information with each other about their encounters, and a culture will then develop among the game-generated characters, a culture that includes references to you and your style of fighting.

In this kind of game — one in which the behavior of creatures evolves with experience — the same creatures will become progressively more difficult to defeat because they'll be wiser and craftier each time you tangle with them. And they'll invent new approaches on the fly to defeat you. Monsters will even learn to generate the appropriate player-killer-style verbal taunts, insults, and responses while attacking you. And, because of this ability to continuously change and adapt, Player vs. Environment games will become almost indistinguishable from Player vs. Player games in their subtlety, complexity, and ferocity.

The third inevitable development is the mixing of game formats that is picking up steam as MMORPG games begin to hybridize with other forms.

First person shooter (FPS) games — in which players chase each other through dungeons with malevolent intent — are already incorporated into some MMORPG designs. And *strategy game* design is finding its way into MMORPG worlds that are filling up with game-generated minions and hirelings.

At the moment, most MMORPG games allow pets, creatures that can be mesmerized into following orders. And some games even allow the hypnosis of other player characters. But, in the new mixed strategy/ MMORPG games, players will be able to build armies of hypnotizable (programmable) NPCs that they can order around. These lackeys will be earned through experience or bought for virtual coin at a local indentured servant market. And players will be able to treat the hoards of programmable creatures as chattel, assigning some to attack enemy camps as others bring in crops, wool, wood, and ore in a far more complex fashion than in a standard RTS game.

At the same time, MMORPG outer space games will meld with *flight simulators* to allow players to do more than just zap themselves through wormholes and appear on the surfaces of distant planets. Space games will become less like multiple-planet medieval games and more like genuine intergalactic endeavors where some players will choose to live their virtual lives never setting foot on terra firma.

Process games are influencing MMORPG games as well, especially MMORPGs that hope to attract women to their player ranks. Process games emphasize context and nonviolent interactions between characters. The most popular standalone electronic game in the world, The Sims, emphasizes just this kind of process, the process of living, and has proven to be far more popular with women than shoot-em-ups.

In MMORPGs built with this milieu in mind, player characters will be able to engage in tasks that are relevant to the game but more process-oriented and creative. Music, for example, with its ability to heal other players or soothe savage beasts, will be used by players who compose melodies from scratch using their keyboards. Some of these tunes will be carried around by the players and used as identifying personal theme songs. Certain monsters will be coded to respond to particular musical phrases (arpeggios, ostinati, a reggae beat perhaps) and what was once a process of hitting a creature on the head with a club until it succumbed will become one of musical experimenting to find the style that tames the critter and forces it to give up its loot.

The physical customization of the world will also improve. Players will be given 3D sculpting tools — not just parts menus — to design and mold their own characters' appearances, their domiciles, and their own creatures — which they'll then program to defend or attack their fellow players. And players will be able to create their own landscapes and add them to the game world for other players to traverse. The whole process of game development will become a more collaborative effort between players and developers. And most of what players see in the game landscape — including monsters — will eventually be created by the players themselves, not the developers.

Sports games will also be folded into MMORPGs to finally liberate characters from the constraint of doing nothing but running and hitting. And quests in such games will include more than just blasting a dozen monsters to seize control of a dungeon. The character will, instead, skateboard down a flowing stalactite slope to reach the glowing nuggets, rock-climb out of the cave to its mountaintop entrance, paraglide into the jungle to redeem the nuggets for experience points, and race a Formula One car out of the forest to escape the flying monkeys that harass everyone who completes the quest.

In time, it will become difficult to separate pure MMORPG games from other types of games as all of the different genres begin to borrow from each other and converge online.

The fourth inevitable development is the splintering of MMORPG environments into hundreds of different forms, each aimed at a very particular audience. The tools for developing games are now available as freeware, and it's possible for a few developers to get together nights and weekends to build a game that appeals to (and makes a profit from) a couple of thousand players. When this practice becomes more widespread, not only will there be military conquest games, space games, and medieval games. There will also be games that are derived from every genre, every mythology, every culture, every demographic, and every time period in history. This includes sex games, teaching games, hospital games, business games, and models-and-makeup games.

Genre games will include 1950s American rock 'n' roll suburb worlds, entirely nocturnal 1940s jazz club hangout worlds, 1930s gangster cities, and holiday MMORPGs just for Christmas, New Year's Eve, Halloween, and Thanksgiving. There will be dime novel westerns, silent movie vamps and tramps worlds, suspenseful gritty private eye neighborhoods, woodsy summer camps, and Wall Street boardroom worlds where characters use merger and acquisition agreements as weapons in hostile takeovers against competing corporations.

There will be hiphop worlds full of warring lyrics, drug deals, prison stints, and public assassinations. And, obviously, there will be mafia worlds where the wiseguy allegiance system rankings will include soldier, made man, underboss, capo, consigliere, and godfather, and where the game tokens will feature horse's heads, fish wrapped in newspaper, cement overshoes, and an end user licensing agreement you cannot refuse.

Culturally rooted games will include not only the obvious samurais and shoguns, outlaws and sheriffs, and imperialists and freedom fighters, but also games drawn from the real world's various subcultures. Gnarly surfer dude worlds will be created full of rogue black-suited wave stealers who rake their long board skags over the backs of paddling enemies. Winning surf guilds in these worlds will control the primo machine-wave point breaks. And losing beach guilds will be exiled to crumbly chop or wild unsurfable close-outs that stand up, never barrel, and mow down anyone who goes near them even with a tow-in.

Every special interest group will have its own world as well. There will be historical/religious worlds based on the Old Testament in which you can smite heathens, raze the walls of Jericho, defeat a hundred Goliaths a day, and exchange as many body parts as you like in the Eye for an Eye and Tooth for a Tooth Quest. And there will even be political viewpoint worlds, similar to *Special Force*, the non–MMORPG game developed by Hizbollah in Lebanon to redress what they see as the overabundance of military games in which the Westerners always win.

There will be Gypsy worlds, circus worlds, Swiss alpine worlds, Civil War worlds, and worlds for model-train aficionados, Bronze Age reenactors, and ballroom dancers.

And product placements will worm their way into many of these games, just as they have into movies. You'll be able to buy Mr. Zog's Sex Wax for your stick in the Surfer's Paradise World and enter the Glory Hole in the San Francisco '70s Gay Bathhouse World. Your characters will eat Official Astronaut Ice Cream in the Solar System Exploration World. And they'll wear official Pumpkin Skull Brand fire-retardant masks in the Halloween World.

Demographic games will include worlds designed not only for religious people of particular faiths, but also post-menopausal women and nonnative speakers of English. There will be worlds exclusively for pre-teen girls (think pink and purple), newly retired men (complete with sleeveless undershirts, trousers pulled up to the nipples, and the Putting Screws in Jars in the Basement quest), and a world for the recently divorced (plenty of cathartic pummeling to be expected in that one).

Event-driven games will feature every war in recorded history recreated in the game universe, complete with camp followers, USO shows, resistance movements, and POW camps. There will be famous sporting events, including every Olympic sport, the World Series, and the World Cup. Even recent news events will trigger the creation of impromptu games in which you participate in whatever action is currently in the headlines. You'll be able to expose government corruption, defeat terrorists, put up your own candidate to replace the president, or rehabilitate the national economy.

Every new Hollywood movie and many television shows may eventually feature a play-along MMORPG game tie-in as well. Obvious ones include kung-fu films, spy movies, murder mysteries, and goofball comedies. But old movies may be resurrected in the game world as well. You'll be able to play Rhett Butler at Tara in *Gone with the Wind* or become one of hundreds of Cowardly Lions; Moes, Larrys, or Curlies; or Men of Steel.

The fifth obvious development will be the migration of MMORPGs out of the pure entertainment space and into educational and business uses.

Many people who love MMORPG games bemoan the amount of time they spend on them because they carry away from the games nothing that can be applied to the real world. They spend thousands of hours looking up how to perform quests, where to find certain items, when to assault castles, the meanings of cryptic inscriptions, the weaknesses of particular monsters, the proper protocols for forming an allegiance, the background and powers of certain objects, and the kinds of exchange goods necessary for the purchase of cottages. But all of that information is useless outside of the game world.

To preserve the spirit of MMORPGs but resolve this disposable knowledge problem, developers will build games that introduce useful information into MMORPGs. In this way, the addictive power of the games will be harnessed for genuine education.

One of the worlds I've been designing, for example, focuses on foreign language acquisition, chemistry, math, civics, meteorology, animal behavior, ecology, and genetics. In this world:

- The inscriptions that lead to dungeon prizes are not written in a made-up Orkish language but in actual Hanzi/Kanji, so players begin to learn actual Chinese/Japanese characters as they play.
- The directions given by an NPC are presented not in an invented

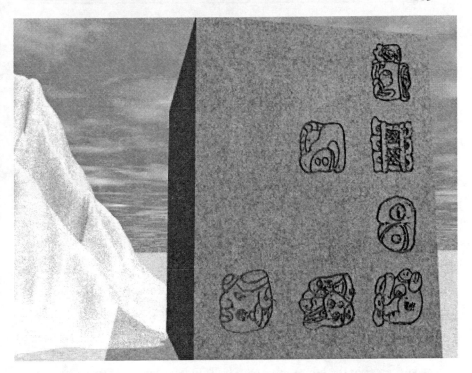

The stela has to be translated by the player based on the player's Mayan lexicon (earned in another quest). The glyphs say, "Och-ch'een-na. (Enter cave.) T'abay-yi-tsam. (Ascend throne.) Chum-mu. (Be seated.) Ajaw Bahlam, yu-xu-lu. (Lord Jaguar carved this.)" A player who then enters the cave and sits on the throne is rewarded with uber-loot, a quest item, and a clue to another mission.

gestural language but in American Sign Language. (Vendors sign the types of goods they sell, so you need to learn the signs from the visual dictionary before getting your equipment. And some quest rumormongers give their spiels entirely in sign, so you have to look up the gestures in your sign lexicon (part of the game's GUI) before commencing the quest.

• The chemical formulas required to mix a potion in the game are based not on alchemical herbs and mystical essences but on the elements of the actual periodic table whose known reactions have to be understood in order to create the proper spells. (At the simplest level even such real-world information as acid + base = salt can yield useful results in the game.)

An enchanter in the Educational MMORPG uses a chameleon spell to change her own appearance while mesmerizing an Ant Lord with bubbles created according to formulas that relate to viscosity.

- Puzzles take the form of equations that relate directly to the task at hand (for example, calculating how much pressure has to be applied to a limestone temple doorway in order to wedge it out of the way without breaking the lintel and collapsing the ceiling).
- Meteorology gets some play as well. One quest can be commenced only when the barometer is falling and the dew point is rising.
- And many of the creatures act in the same way as their counterparts in the real world. Ungulates such as bison and wildebeest stampede when provoked (so you can drive them over a cliff) while baboon troops scatter and reform.

The trick in such worlds is to build in all of this project-based learning in such a way that it is invisible. There's no rote memorization involved, only active learning. Players acquire knowledge *in context* and *in pursuit of immediate goals*—just as they do in any ordinary MMORPG. They don't memorize and disgorge the periodic table onto a test paper. They figure out which element combines with which other elements in order to create the compound they need to defeat a particular monster. They don't sit in a language lab mindlessly parroting ridiculous "Où est la plume de ma tante?" (French: "Where is the pen of my aunt?") and "Kore-wa watashi-no empitsu desu" (Japanese: "This is my pencil") textbook sentences. They see and hear someone speaking another language and have to decode that speaker's words in order to complete the quest, make money, find their way, and flourish. Learning is done in the service of game goals, just as it is in regular MMORPGs. Players are immersed in an environment and the learning is done incidentally through problem solving.

The amount of information learned in this kind of game is the same hefty amount acquired in any MMORPG. Players have to figure out everything they need to know to feed themselves, stay safe, rise in experience, acquire the items they covet, and navigate the world around them. But, in this game, they do it by picking up knowledge that actually has some use in the real world. The game's design is not meant to trick people into learning. It's meant to give players the tools they need to succeed in the *virtual* world, but tools that may be useful in the *real* world as well.

General education is not the only way in which these kinds of games will eventually be used, however. MMORPG games are essentially self-contained worlds, no different from the worlds of doughnut shops, hamburger franchises, public school classrooms, brokerage centers, operating rooms, gas stations, fire houses, and insurance offices. And all of these workplace worlds will eventually be recreated in the virtual realm to teach people how to perform in them.

Many kinds of employee training, consequently, will be done *in virtuo* using corporate and public MMORPG worlds as training grounds. Occupation-specific MMORPGs will allow firefighters to assess different kinds of fires, oil refinery workers to walk through and adjust chemical flows, archeologists to map and plan digs, civil defense officials to devise escape routes, and emergency room interns to triage patients.

And, because MMORPGs can present complex information to

An NPC quest initiator in the nocturnal desert quizzes passersby in Japanese in the Educational MMORPG. Players earn a lexicon of Japanese spoken and written words in a previous quest and must use it to decipher the questions of the Scary Kabuki Girl to move on to the next realm.

thousands of people simultaneously, game engines can also be used as front ends for all kinds of databases. Just as they now act as GUI front-ends for immense item, monster, and character databases, MMORPG game engines will eventually be used as front-ends for corporate, government, and medical databases that involve 3D information (such as walkthroughs of medical procedures or exploded views of medical instruments). You'll not only be able to see the operation you're about to have done performed in front of you in the MMORPG hospital, you'll be able to perform it yourself.

And the impact of MMORPGs won't be limited to the workaday world because the physical architecture of a MMORPG environment is up to the developer. It is possible to build universes on a galactic scale for astronomers, or on a molecular scale for physicists exploring sub-atomic particle theory. In fact, MMORPGs are perfect for providing a

Bubble dome settlements in the foothills of the lunar region known as the Altai Scarp in the Lunar Exploration MMORPG.

virtual workspace for places that are difficult for ordinary people to see or get to.

The second of my two world-development projects, for example, is a Lunar Colonization MMORPG. In it, there are databases of the items that make life on a moon with no atmosphere and one-sixth gravity possible (space suits, oxygen rebreathers, tinted plastic sun shields, etc.). There are also shelters to construct (temporary inflatable quonset huts at the beginning, tubular extruded glass hogans made from the local silicates later on). There are opportunities to produce solar energy, smelt nickel ore into metal, grow food in greenhouses (using trade skills), and melt subterranean polar ice for water (used for drinking and for hydrolysis into hydrogen and oxygen fuel). And there are limitations to overcome through a gradual process of bootstrapping and leveling.

This game's design offers all of the standard elements of a MMORPG, but the goal behind it is not to bludgeon trolls and cast spells. It is to devise a way of living on and adapting to the moon's unique constraints and opportunities. It's a simulator for future lunar colonization.

At level 1 your character learns to walk in low G. By level 3 you can build moisture- and energy-recapture suits. By level 5, cartographic expeditions become possible. At level 10, you can construct portable fuel cells to extend your exploration into the distant maria. At level 15, bioassays of your crew are within your reach. At level 20, devising autonomous solar array production facilities that use the energy gleaned from the sun to robotically manufacture and install new panels allows you to build an independent town. And, by level 30, spaceport design and development are within your grasp.

These kinds of specialized worlds, created by groups with particular interests will sprout across the global Internet drawing players from professionals in certain fields, students hoping to work in those fields, and inspired amateurs who love the subject matter enough to immerse themselves in it on a daily basis.

And all of this development will tie in with the last inevitable development in MMORPGs. The tools necessary for creating a MMORPG will be put into the hands of everyone. Just as photographic manipulation software and nonlinear film-editing software have descended in price from millions of dollars to dozens of dollars, MMORPG development systems will drop from a level at which only the largest corporations can afford to build and field games to a level at which every person at home can build one. And these will be full-spectrum games, complete with hand-tooled characters, AI-driven monsters, multiuser network interfaces, large item databases, complex landscapes, and rich and compelling lore.

The first forays into this area are already occurring in three different formats. One is the game-with-tools idea in which companies provide both a game and the tools by which players can adjust the game or build their own games. The Aurora Toolset game development package that comes with Neverwinter Nights from Bioware is a good example. The tool set includes everything necessary to develop modules and entirely new games using the same landscape components, items, buildings, monsters, music, and AI code used in the creation of the original game.

A variation on this approach is that of Linden Lab, the developers of Second Life, an online world in which the creative content development tools are all brought inside the game, allowing players themselves to design and build their own houses, work out their own competitions, design and tailor their own clothes, and construct and animate their own bodies — all from scratch.

The second approach is to provide the software necessary to build whole games from the ground up. The Torque Game Engine from the independent game developers group at Garage Games, and open source (free) game engines such as Cube 3D, Crystalspace, and World Forge, all work on this model.

These tools offer anyone with a PC the chance to develop their own games complete with landscapes to run through, buildings to inhabit, lore that establishes context, AI-based monsters to battle, NPC vendors to trade with, items to own and wield, quests to go on, and characters to play.

There is a limitation on the number of simultaneous players who can use most of these handmade worlds online (64 to 128 players seems to be common). So the games are often mMORPGs (minimally multiplayer), rather than MMORPGs. But for most home game developers this limitation is irrelevant.

These kinds of tools are already beginning to yield worlds that feature interesting and innovative features:

- quests in which the prize is to write the next section of the game's lore or design the next quest
- monsters named after mean old girlfriends and nasty ex-husbands
- new trade skills that include nose-mining (to collect mucus plugs that stick monsters to the ground), scent tracking (to sniff out gold deposits hidden in subterranean vaults), and farting as a superpower
- navigational devices such as maze strings (a la Theseus in the Minotaur's cave) and bread crumb trails (a la Hansel and Gretel)
- and literary casinos created by the *otaku literati* in which you win items by correctly answering questions about the characters and events in various fantasy novels.

When everyone can build a MMORPG, the dynamics of the game business will begin to shift. At first, corporate game developers will study the homemade games and "borrow" every innovative feature they find there. Home developers won't have the resources to sue large corporations over intellectual property, so the big companies will just co-opt any feature the home developers invent — while they themselves will sue home developers who use what the corporations proclaim as proprietary ideas and techniques.

Eventually, though, some developers will simply outrun the corporations. They'll keep their ideas out of the corporate domain by wrapping them in a GPL (General Public License: an "inverse patent" that can prevent other companies from owning the code). And they'll acquire a reputation for innovation and sophistication among online gamers.

Anyone who thinks it is unreasonable that programmers, writers, and artists will spend thousands of their own hours creating objects, lore, and code for the free use of everyone else in a MMORPG need only look at the astonishing number of hours people have already put into developing and distributing bots, macros, plug-ins, and skins for existing MMORPG games. When people love what they're doing, they will contribute their time freely. And a successful game doesn't require all ten thousand players to create new items. Only a few clever contributors can have a huge effect on the complexion and complexity of a game.

Keep in mind that there are millions of gamers, programmers, writers, and graphics developers in the real world. And, until now, they've been unable to contribute their creativity to the game universe because they didn't live in one of the half dozen towns around the world where games have traditionally been created. But, once the tools make their way out to the general populace, Linux — the open source operating system — will become the model for MMORPG game development. With free tools, the MMORPG developers will charge only for the content they've created and with little overhead, these MMORPGs will be cheaper to play than the corporate games.

All MMORPG games, even the corporate ones, are also likely to evolve in a direction that allows some kind of customization by the players themselves. And they may end up using the same model as that used for the Dungeons & Dragons board game.

Beginners to D&D, for example, start out by using the canned

Skeletons skating on thin ice, leading the way to a quest in the Educational MMORPG.

"adventure" scripts created by the company. But, as they become more savvy about game play, they begin to experiment with creating their own adventures. In time, the players who discover a talent for devising these scenarios become the adventure creators and dungeon masters for most of the games their group plays.

The same pattern of use is possible in the MMORPG world. Players may initially play the game the developers have written. But as their experience with the game increases, they may add their own features. Eventually, they may even rewrite the game for themselves and their friends on a "virtual server" that identifies each player and selects certain code plug-ins that give one group of players an experience that is different from all others in the game. For some players, then, most of what they see will have been created by the developers, but their unique version of the game will include the landscapes, monsters, and items that they themselves have created for the game.

The only limitation in this brand of collective guerilla game-creation is marketing. Large game worlds have thousands of participants. But encouraging thousands of other people to sign onto your particular world and to then spend years leveling up their characters will require creative viral advertising. So, mini–MMORPGs, demos of the real games, will eventually show up in e-mail as multimedia spam. You'll click to open the mail and you'll be in the game world.

And, just as in the world of filmmaking, access to the tools will become less and less of a limiting factor. The creativity and sophistication of the game along with the developers' ability to distribute their work will be what makes or breaks a MMORPG in the future.

The good news, though, is that once MMORPG game development kits begin to spread around the world, the creative content of the games will explode. At the moment, all corporate games have to be designed with the idea of making big money and attracting huge audiences (40,000 players is often considered the break-even point). As a result, the games all contain the same basic components and are now designed more or less by formula. But when everyone can get into the act, the strictures of corporate control will be lifted. And we'll finally see the true potential of MMORPGs in entertainment, business, science, and education.

Appendix

Online Addiction Organizations

American Academy of Addiction Psychiatry: http://www.aaap.org/

Center for Addiction and Mental Health: http://www.camh.net/

Center for On-line Addiction:
http://www.healthyplace.com/Communities/Addictions/netaddiction/
articles/habitforming.htm

Center for Online and Internet Addiction: http://www.netaddiction.com/

Gameaholics Anonymous: pub45.ezboard.com/fgameaholicsanonymousfrm2

National Center on Addiction and Substance Abuse:
http://www.casacolumbia.org/

On-line Gamers Anonymous: www.olganon.org

MMORPG Information Sites

Mmorpg.com
Mmorpg.net
Mpogd.com
Ogaming.com
Onrpg.com (lists free MMORPGs, free trials, and open betas)
Rpgplanet.com
Rpgvault.ign.com
Stratics.com
Warcy.com

Bibliography

Adams, Douglas. *The Hitchhiker's Guide to the Galaxy.* New York: Ballantine, 1995.

Asher, Mark. "Massive (Multiplayer) Entertainment — Playing Together Online — Yesterday." *Computer Games Magazine,* July 2001. Available at: www.cgonline. com/features/010717-f1-f1.html. A short and selective timeline of multiplayer games.

Brooks, Terry. *The Sword of Shannara.* New York: Ballantine, 1995. Count the startling the similarities to *Lord of the Rings.*

Brown, Margaret Wise. *Goodnight Moon.* New York: Harper Festival, 1991.

Bunyan, John. *Pilgrim's Progress.* New York: Viking, 1965.

"Buying Swords on the Black Market." *Frictionless Insight Archive synopsis of Korea Herald article,* August 12, 2002. Available at: www.frictionlessinsight.com/Archive/ Weekof 2002_08_11.htm. Synopsis of story on NCSoft banning 200,000 accounts for out-of-game trading and being supported by Korean court system.

Castronova, Edward. "Virtual Worlds: A First-Hand Account of Market and Society on the Cyberian Frontier." *CESifo Working Paper Series No. 618,* December 2001. Available at: papers.ssrn.com/sol3/papers.cfm?abstract_id= 294828. Economic report that focuses on the virtual land of Norrath.

CNET Asia Staff. "Thai Government Bans Online Games at Night." *ZDNet UK News,* July 9, 2003. Available at: news.zdnet.co.uk/internet/0,39020369, 2137269,00.htm. Report on Thailand's ban on MMORPG playing.

Dumas, Alexandre. *The Three Musketeers.* New York: Puffin, 2002.

Eddings, David. *Guardians of the West.* New York: Ballantine, 1998.

"Father Admits Guilt in Death of 9-Month-Old." *St. Petersburg Times.* January 3, 2001. Available at: www.sptimes.com/News/010301/TampaBay/Tampa_Bay_briefs.shtml. Death of child at hands of father playing MMORPG.

Feist, Raymond E. *Magician: Apprentice.* New York: Bantam, 1994.

Gluck, Caroline. "South Korea's Gaming Addicts." *BBC News,* November 22, 2002. Available at: news.bbc.co.uk/1/hi/world/asia-pacific/2499957.stm. Report on game addiction and death of addicted player after 86 hours of play.

Goodkind, Terry. *Wizard's First Rule.* New York: Tor, 1997. First book in long Sword of Truth series.

Goodwins, Rupert, and Matt Loney. "In Greece, Use a Gameboy, Go to Jail." *C/Net News.com,* September 3, 2002. Available at: news.com.com/2100-1040-956357.html. Article on Greek government's ban on electronic games.

Goot, Dustin. "Frosty the Painkiller." *Wired Magazine*, October 2003. Article on the use of virtual reality in alleviating pain among burn patients.

Grohol, John M. "Internet Addiction Guide." *Psych Central,* March 2003. Available at: psychcentral.com/netaddiction/. A monograph/review that questions whether Internet addiction even exists.

Harris, Chris. "Could you be addicted to the Internet?" *Hartford Advocate,* 2002. Available at: old.hartfordadvocate.com/articles/onlinejunkies.html. Excellent article on Internet and MMORPG addiction.

Harrison, Harry. *The Stainless Steel Rat.* New York: Orion, 1997.

Haseltine, Eric. "The Unsatisfied Mind." *Discover Magazine*, November 2001. A brief article on the genetics and biology of addictive behavior.

Haydon, Elizabeth. *Rhapsody: Child of Blood.* New York: Tor, 1999.

Herbert, Frank. *Dune.* New York: Ace, 2003.

Jordan, Robert. *The Dragon Reborn.* New York: Tor, 1993.

Kahn, Noor, and H. LeMair. *Twenty Jataka Tales.* London: Inner Dimensions, 1991.

Koike, Kazuo. *Lone Wolf and Cub 1: The Assassin's Road.* New York: Penguin Putnam, 2000.

Lackey, Mercedes. *Werehunter.* New York: Pocket, 1999.

Lao Tzu. *Tao Te Ching.* Translated by Gia-fu Feng and Jane English. New York: Vintage, 1972.

Mackay, Daniel. *The Fantasy Role-Playing Game: A New Performing Art.* Jefferson, NC: McFarland, 2001. A scholarly work on the theatrical elements to be found in role-playing games.

Miller II, Stanley A. "Death of a Game Addict." *Milwaukee Journal Sentinel*, March 31, 2002. Available at: www.jsonline.com/news/state/mar02/31536.asp. Article on man who took his own life after hours of MMORPG playing.

Morris, William. *The Well at World's End.* Holicong, PA: Wildside, 2000. Early fantasy novel used as a model and inspiration by J.R.R. Tolkien. Includes a lord with the name of Gandolf, a horse named Silverfax, and a heroic quest by a Fellowship of Champions.

Nemeth, Andrea. "Addiction to the Web — Examination of Negative Impacts." University of Calgary. Available at: www.ucalgary.ca/~dabrent/380/webproj/addiction.html. Academic overview of Internet addiction, includes short bibliography.

Nix, Garth. *Sabriel.* New York: Harper Trophy, 1997.

Nordoff, Charles, and James Hall. *Mutiny on the Bounty: A Novel.* Boston: Back Bay, 1989.

Orzack, Maressa Hecht. "Computer Addiction: What Is It?" *Psychiatric Times* 15, no. 8 (August 1998). Available at: www.psychiatrictimes.com/p980852.html. Discussion of tolerance, withdrawal, and compulsive use as indicators of online addiction.

Pratchett, Terry. *Hogfather.* New York: Harper Torch, 1999. Twenty-first novel in the Discworld series.

Sandoval, Greg. "Sony to Ban Sale of Online Characters from Its Popular Gaming Sites." *C/Net News.com,* April 10, 2000. Available at: news.com.com/2100-1017_3-239052.html?tag=mainstry. Article announcing Sony's ban on sales of Everquest virtual items and characters.

Scheeres, Julia. "The Quest to End Game Addiction." *Wired.* December 5, 2001. Available at: www.wired.com/news/holidays/0,1882,48479,00.html. Article on game widows and game addiction.

"Terror Game Available." *Herald Sun (Victoria, Australia),* June 3, 2003. Available at: heraldsun.news.com.au/common/story_page/0,5478,6539982% 5E421,00.html. Archived article on game developed by Hizbollah.

Tolkien, J.R.R. *The Hobbit, or There and Back Again.* New York: Houghton Mifflin, 1999. A work of genius. Far better than *Lord of the Rings.* And an inspiration for medieval MMORPG developers everywhere.

Weis, Margaret, and Tracy Hickman. *Dragons of Autumn Light.* Los Angeles: Wizards of the Coast, 2003. First book in the Dragonlance trilogy.

Index

Accomplishment in MMORPGs 76–80

Adopting a character role 20

Age of Empires 22

AI programming 172

All-carrot-no-stick principle 30, 34, 39, 45

Allegiance groups 34

Alternative history as lore 105

Anarchy Online 103, 104, 130–32

Ancient Egypt as a vitual world 109

Arneson, Dave 19

Arranging one's daily schedule to play 68

Arthurian romance 20

Asheron's Call 23, 102, 104

Asheron's Call 2 104, 119–22

Attraction to MMORPGs: reasons for 62–66

Augmenters and revealers 153

Avatars 25, 58; as branch offices of the self 59; as buddies 61; as offspring 60

Baggins, Bilbo 47

Becoming a fictional character 61

Bots 35, 114, 155, 156

Bragg, Tony Lamont 17

Brooks, Terry 47

Camelot 19

Campbell, Joseph 95

Cartels 35; names of 35

Castronova, Edward 15

Character: appearance 25; creation 28; defined 25; keeping track of health in 20; name as a reflection of self 26; names 26; profession or class 25

Character animation 170–71

Character appearance 52–58; and benefits of female gender 54; as a tool and strategy 57; vs. player age 52; vs. player gender 54

Character behavior: as an art form 83; modelling real human development 85

Character names: clever 48; and corporate intellectual property 50; and enchantment 52; from fantasy novels 47; from history and literature 47; humorous 49; lyrical 48; from the media 49; national 50; Sugar Glider 51; violent 50

Characters: created by the player 25; Creature 27; defined traits and roles 20; as exemplars of player attitudes 59; mage type 26; manifesting the ideals of the players 61; melee type 26; Non-player (NPC) 27; Player (PC) 27; ranger type 26

Chat spew 23

City of Heroes 101, 105–6

Civilization 22

Clans 35

Codemasters 126

Collaborative story-telling 18

Columbus, Christopher 72

Computer as mediator of personal interactions 22
Cook, Captain 72
Creativity 80–84
Creatures 27
Cryptic Studios 105
Crystalspace 166, 189
Cube 3D 166, 189

D&D Online 149
Dark Age of Camelot 15, 103, 129–30
Darkfall 111–13
Death of MMORPG players 17
Definitions of game slang 165
The Dietrichsage 71
Differences in treatment of male and female characters 54–56
Digital Equipment Corporation 9
Dragon Empires 126–27
Dungeon master 20
Dungeons & Dragons 19, 190

Earth and Beyond 104, 106–8
Economies 36–40
Economy: player-based 120
Eddings, David 47
eGenesis 109
Elements of MMORPG culture 24
E-mail games 21
Endless Ages 103, 149
Erasing the line between myth and reality 33
Erikson, Leif 19
EverQuest 15, 23, 102, 139–41; death 17; economy 15
Experience points 27; as an addiction system 28; in relation to level 27
Experiments: creating art 82; creating female characters 55; educational MMORPG 182; lunar colonization MMORPG 187; newbies and money 39; virtual reality 10

Factions 35
Fan fiction 155
Fan sites 151–56; characteristics 152; specific sites 194
Fantasy Fiction 19
Farming 16
Feist, Raymond 47

Female characters 54, 55, 57
Female players 17, 52, 56, 70, 73; helpful 56; as male characters 56
Final Fantasy 23
Final Fantasy XI 15, 149
First person shooter games 43
Flamimg 58
Funcom 131
Future of MMORPGs: in education and business 182; features introduced by small developers 189; graphics quality 177; inexpensive tools 188; mixing of game formats 178; multimedia spam 192; sophistication of AI 177; splintering of MMORPG environments 180

Game art 168–70
Game characteristics: balance 101; ethos 104; graphics 101; number of players 103; skills and leveling 103; social constraints 102; type of developer 103
Game characters: as extensions of the self 58; as friends 61; as manifestations of player ideals 61
Game databases 173
Game design 167–68
Game economy based on real money 16, 133
Game friendship vs. real friendship 59, 74
Game life as a learning experience 91
Game testing 174
Game within a game 115
Gameful employment 97
Ganking 42
Garage Games 166
Gilgamesh 19
Goodkind, Terry 47
Goodnight Moon 99
GPL 190
Growth without failure 28–30
Guilds 34–36; and communism 35; and friendship 34
Gygax, Gary 19

Harrison, Harry 47
Haydon, Elizabeth 47
Herbert, Frank 47

Holmes, Sherlock 49
Horizons 150

Ibn Battuta 72
Instinctive attraction to MMORPGs 72–73
Interactive maps 153
Isometric view 101, 136, 141

Jack o'lantern sculptures 81
Jaleco Entertainment 125
Jataka Tales 87
JC Entertainment 125
Jordan, Robert 47
Jung, Carl 86

Kent, Clark 98

Lackey, Mercedes 47
LAN parties 159
Landscape fraught with peril 20
Lascaux Cave as a MMORPG 18
Legend of Zelda 23
Leveling treadmill 102
Lewis and Clark 72
Lineage 14, 15, 17, 101, 141–43
Lol 160
Lone gunslinger 43
Lord of the Rings 148
Lore 69–71; and fan fiction 71
Lost Continents 122–25
Lowbie 160
LucasArts 144
Lying about time spent playing 68

MacCvs 166
Macro development kits 153
Macros and bots 156–58; creating a macro 157; script 157; types of bots 157
Mad King Ludwig 71
Mafia dating services 35
Magellan 72
Mario 58
Maslow's Hierarchy of Needs 86
Masterless samurai 43
Matrix Online 150
Meaningful relationships without maintenance 34
Medieval craftsmen's guild 35

Mercantile-warrior 37
Middle Earth Online 104, 148–49
Milkshape 166
MindArk 135
Minimally multiplayer games 189
Mission clocks 106
MMORPG: attraction and addiction 62–99; creation 166–76; culture 24–45; currency 15; evolution 13–23; future development 177–92; game reviews 100–50; personal experience 1–11; player-created spin-offs 150–65; player psychology 46–61
MMORPG addiction: and creativity 80; and displacement 76; and the feeling of accomplishment 76; genetic predisposition 67; and guaranteed protection from catastrophe 25; and human needs 66; names indicating 49; percentage of MMORPG players who are addicts 66; and primal instincts 72; as a result of never falling back 28; as a result of protection from the savagery of real life 29; as a result of triumph without risk 44; and the sense of urgency 78; as a substitute for more harmful addictions 94; symptoms of 67; via environmental manipulation 66; vs. television viewing 95
MMORPG life: as a mood alterant 68; as the perfect job 96–99
MMORPG players: judged by their characters' abilities 62; misconceptions about 76
MMORPGs: and the absence of failure 30; attractions for female players 56, 70, 179; banned by the government 16; benefits of playing 14; from the Buddhist, Hindu, Taoist perspective 87; as a business 14; cost of playing 15, 101; daily progress in 24; death as a result of playing 17; defined 13; as enhancements to real life 65; as enveloping worlds 62; as escapism 64; the first ones 23; as a form of religion 91; as a growth experience 29; and guaranteed protection from catastrophe 28; as improvers of real

human character 90; legal questions 15; length of time played 13; as mechanisms of spiritual growth 87; negative consequences of playing 14; number of players 15; and pain reduction 93; revenue generated from 15; as salves for real life misery 63; as a shared passion 73; as a societal force 16; in South Korea and Thailand 16; as substitutes for real life 64; vs. videogames 14, 15, 25, 28, 29, 70, 85, 175
Morris, William 19
Moyers, Bill 95
MUDs 20
Mutants as characters 105
Mythic Entertainment 130

Naive physics 171
Names of characters 46–52
NCSoft 15, 141
Neglecting friends to play 67
NeL 166
Neocron 127–29
Neuschwanstein Castle 71
NeverWinter Nights 188
Nevrax 119
The Nibelungenlied 71
Nix, Garth 47
Noah 19
NPCs 27
nucleus accumbens 67
Numeroff, Laura 49

Odysseus 19
One-person-becomes-one-character games 22
Online addiction websites 193
ORIGIN Systems 136

Parker, Jay 17
Persistent state universe 29
Philbrick and Philbrick 49
Pilgrim's Progress 87
Pirates of the Burning Sea 150
Player associations 34
Player behavior: cheating and hurting 39; competitive 38; coquettish 56; destructive 41; detestable 36; falsifying the self 54; female, older 56; female, younger 56; good and evil 59; greybeards 53; mercantile-warriors 37; newbies 39; preying on weakness 54; rejoicing over pain and death 41; similarity to character behavior 58–61; stages 10; territorial disputes 41; thrill killing 43; vs. character behavior 59; worldview 10
Player characters: as extreme versions of the self 60; housing the ego of the player 61; representing a fresh start in life 63
Player killer: duels 42; guild names 42
Player killer society: and fascism 41
Player killing 40–45; as a reflection of real life 44
Player-owned items 16
Players from: Australia 50; Austria 71; Boston 82; California 36; Chicago 35; Colorado 33; Copenhagen 2; Denmark 50; Europe 6; Florida 17; France 50; Hawaii 95; Indiana 76; Massachusetts 4; Minnesota 32; Missouri 36; Pittsburgh 109; Quebec 6; South Korea 17; Sweden 16; Thailand 17; Washington 17; Western Canada 3; Wisconsin 17
Plug-ins 153, 155
Polo, Marco 72
Pratchett, Terry 47
Priest 125–26
Private game zones 123
Programming a game 171–73
Project Entropia 132–35
Pulp fiction as a game venue 122

Quake and *Doom* 43
QuArk 166
Quest types: FedEx 30; fetch 30; lore 32; mail run 30; marathon 32; multipart 31; orienteering 32; player 33; riddle 31; scavenger hunt 31; shrunken head 41; slaughter 31; title 32; treasure 31; zombie 79
Quests 28–34; with adjustable parameters 131; attractions of 33; inserting a player into the narrative 33; and mateship 33

Race 25; types of in a MMORPG 25; wars 41
Ragnarok Online 15, 150
Ramayana 19
Razorwax AS 111
Reactors 124
Reakktor.com 127
Realtime strategy games 22, 101
Red dots 42
Redefining the self 63
Religion 85–92
Revenge databases 42
Ronin 18
RPGs 23
Rubies of Eventide 150
Rumormongers 30

Saga of Ryzom 104, 117–19
SciFi games 106, 130, 132, 144
Scope of MMORPG landscapes 63
Second Life 102, 150, 189
Siegfried and Kriemhild 71
Skills and skill credits 26
Slang 10, 159–65
Social interaction in MMORPGs 73–76
Sony 15, 17
Sony Online Entertainment 144
Sound and music 173–74
Spiritual development in MMORPG players 85–92
Spoilers 152
Stages of a character's life 77–80; abandonment and return cycle 78; The Adventurer 77; The Anonymous Noob 77; The Explorer 77; Miles Gloriosus 77; The Penurious Warrior 77; The Power Leveler 77; The Sage Advisor 78; vs. stages of real life 86; The Weary Traveler 78

Star Wars Galaxies 15, 104, 143–48
State preserver programs 154
Stonehenge 81
Story circles 18
Stress relief as an attraction 92–96

A Tale in the Desert 102, 103, 108–11
Tolkien, J. R. R. 19, 47, 148
Toons 25
Toontown 101, 113–17
Torque Engine 166, 189
Tribes 34
Turbine Engineering 119, 148
Turn sheets 21

Ultima Online 15, 23, 101, 135–39
University of Washington 93

The Valkyries 71
Vampire slayer, Buffy 98
Vandelay, Art 49
Verant Interactive 139
Villainous players 37
Violence 3–4
Virtual experience with no ending 22
Virtual reality 9; research 82

Walt Disney Imagineering VR Studio 114
Weis and Hickman 47
Westwood Studios 107
WinCvs 166
Wooley, Shawn 17
World Forge 166, 189
World of Warcraft 150
Worldcraft 166
Written adventures 20

Zhang He 72